lus



# Banned!

*Tom Paine, This Was Your Life*

by

## James Watson

Resource Material by

Rachel O'Neill

Series Consultant

Stephen Cockett

Published by Collins Educational, an imprint of HarperCollins*Publishers* Ltd, 77–85 Fulham Palace Road, London W6 8JB





First published 2003

ISBN 000 713 559 9



British Library Cataloguing in Publication Data

A catalogue record for this book is available from the British Library.

**Acknowledgements**
The following permissions to reproduce material are gratefully acknowledged:

*Illustrations:* p98, James Watson; p100, Hulton Getty

*Text extracts:* 'Nurseries fit electronic tags to children' © Sophie Goodchild and Claire Newbon. First published in *The Independent* 26 May 2002. Used with permission; 'Library finger printing' © John Naughton, first published in *The Observer* 28 July 2002. Used with permission from The Guardian and Observer Syndication Group.

Whilst every effort has been made to contact the copyright holders, this has not proved possible in every case.

Design by Nigel Jordan
Cover design by Chi Leung
Cover photograph courtesy Craig van der Lende/Getty Images
Commissioning Editors: Helen Clark and Isabelle Zahar
Editor: Mark Dudgeon

Production: Katie Morris
Typeset by Jordan Publishing Design, Salisbury
Printed and bound in Thailand by Imago

For permission to perform this play, please allow plenty of time and contact: Permissions Department, HarperCollins*Publishers*, 77–85 Fulham Palace Road, London W6 8JB. Tel. 0208 307 4303.

# Contents



**KEY**

71–74 / 71–74 cross-reference between playscript and teaching resources.

H in resources = activity suitable for homework.

# *Cast in order of appearance*

**Jethro Jackson** History master, probationary teacher; popular with his students; form master for 11C.

## FORM 11C

**Tony** Lively, up-front character, witty; ready to 'mix' it verbally or physically.

**Russell** Though labelled with a criminal record and reputation has become more thoughtful as a result of his growing friendship with ***Lysette***. A central character in the play.

**Imran** Amiable, good sense of humour which he uses as a defence against racial taunts; feels secure in the friendship of other members of 11C.

**Denise** Fair minded and tolerant; shows a soft spot for ***Julian***, the Prefect and editor of the school magazine, who to others in 11C is the villain of the piece.

**Celine** Just as ***Imran's*** Pakistani background opens him to comment, in a similar way Celine's physical attractiveness – her 'glamour' – prompts responses; she in turn responds with sharp but humorous comments.

**Sonja** Never quite up with the conversation, but always ready to toss in a comment that reveals both her difficult background and her gift – of which she seems to be unaware – for the absurd.

**Mitchell** Whether Mitchell is genuinely gay is something the others are indifferent about but it suits him to be casually, humorously and sometimes provocatively open about it.

**Lysette** Central character of the play, Lysette is editor of the controversial Form 11C section of the school magazine and author of the article that has caused such a rumpus in the school, 'Pitt School is Pants!' Though a sceptical person, she is also passionate about a number of concerns.

## OTHER CHARACTERS

**Hector Lester** Headmaster, William Pitt School. A mixture of the authoritarian and the stressed humanitarian. Genuinely terrified of the imminent inspection of the school and mortified by the comments in the article written by ***Lysette***.

**Mrs. Draper** School Secretary. Pampers Mr. Lester, but most of her comments suggest a sense of irony.

**Lorna Bolton** English teacher. Young, new to the job; her ideals concerning education and the treatment of her pupils always seem to run counter to the expectations of those in authority.

**Julian Hicks** Prefect, very much an 'A-stream' student; editor of the school magazine, 'Forward', with a rosy professional future ahead of him. Good looking enough to attract ***Denise*** in particular. Plays the game at both ends: diplomatic with those in authority, tolerant and friendly with the 'rebels' of Form 11C. Essentially an opportunist.

**Thomas Paine** The greatest Englishman – ever. Author of *The Rights of Man*. His appearance at William Pitt School generates a crisis because ***Mr. Lester*** is convinced that he is a Schools' Inspector in disguise.

**Voices 1 and 2** Members of the audience for the TV programme, 'Tom Paine, This Was Your Life'. They turn out, as this scene evolves, into secret service agents carrying firearms.

## MINOR CHARACTERS

**Julius Caesar**

**Henry VIII**

**Mrs. Edmund Burke**

**Angel**

**George Washington**

**Jailer**

**Lady Testard, Chair of School Governors**

**A Reporter**

**Madame Bonneville**

# *Banned!*

## *Tom Paine, This Was Your Life*

### Scene 1

*Year 11C of William Pitt School has just assembled and* ***Mr. Jethro Jackson****, History teacher, is calling the register. The stage design should permit maximum flexibility – no desks, just a series of sturdy boxes a metre or so square, half a metre deep, suitable for actors to sit on, as in class, or to be arranged, stacked or cleared away as appropriate. Two pairs of large step-ladders can be used with a plank to create a seat, or actors can simply sit on the steps.*

*The following exchanges are taken at speed.*

**JACKSON** Harding.

**TONY** *stands up, gives a quick triumphal gesture to the audience* Tony will do, Sir, it's more friendly.

**JACKSON** Just answer Yes.

**TONY** Present and incorrect, Sir. (*sits down*)

**JACKSON** Hargreaves, Hebden and Holden – where are they?

**RUSSELL** Gone fishin', Sir.

**JACKSON** Spare me the dimwit, will you, Morgan?

**RUSSELL** Russell, Sir, it sounds more friendly. (*he stands up, flexes a bicep towards the audience*) Russell, me big bad boy.

**JACKSON** Jayasingh.

**RUSSELL** Stumped Wasir Amen, bowled Wakir Braces.

**JACKSON** Russell, cut it!

**IMRAN** *stands, plays an elegant off drive with imaginary cricket bat* Straight four, all along the ground, Sir.

**Jackson** Answer Yes.

**Imran** Yes Sir, England fifteen all out, Pakistan nine hundred for no wicket.

**Tony** What do you expect when the umpires are all Pakis?

**Imran** *sits. Good naturedly* I didn't hear that.

**Jackson** Denise?

**Denise** *stands, gives the audience a modest bow* Yes, Mr. Jackson, what's left of me after last night.

**Jackson** What happened?

**Denise** I was sexually molested.

**Russell** In yer dreams.

**Denise** It's true.

**Jackson** If you want to talk to me about it in private, Denise, see me at break.

***Denise** sits.*

**Tony** Don't you trust him, Den – he might verbally molest you and there's nothing worse.

**Jackson** Celine?

**Russell** 'Ey, Sir – why's it surnames for males an' nice Denise an' Celine for danglies?

**Jackson** Russell, you're not present until I read your name out on the register.

**Russell** Y'er not answerin' my question, JackoSir.

**Jackson** Celine?

**Celine** *stands, preens, does a pirouette for the benefit of the audience* Yes Mr. Jackson.

**Tony** Ask her if she was sexually molested, Sir. We'd believe *her*.

*Cheers from the males.*

**Celine** Shut your face. What's it with these kids with one ball between them, Mr. Jackson? (*she sits*) Aren't there no laws about that kind of comment?

**Jackson** Moon?

**Mitchell** *stands, preens even more outrageously than Celine, then freezes into provocative pose* Shining as ever, Sir. You can molest me any time, day or night.

**Jackson** *staying calm* Answer Yes or Sir, Mitch, or we'll be here till Domesday.

**Mitchell** *coyly* Well if you put it like that, Sir – Y-e-s. (*he sits*)

**Tony** We're not doing that Domesday Book thing again, are we Sir? It's worse than watching paint dry.

**Celine** It wasn't as boring as the Dead Sea Scrawls, though.

**Jackson** Scrolls, Celine. The Dead Sea Scrolls.

**Celine** All the same to me, Sir.

**Jackson** Russell?

**Russell** My name's Morgan, Sir. Not present.

**Jackson** So it's an apparition I see before me?

**Russell** I'm 'ere in body, JackoSir, but not in spirit.

**Imran** *stands, makes a big sign of a heart, droops his head and shakes it* He's missing Lysette, Sir. He's got the hots for her. (*sits, nodding his head in **Russell's** direction*)

**Jackson** *genuinely interested* That right, Russ?

**Russell** My private passions are my concern.

**Jackson** Yes, when they're not plastered all over the front page of the local rag.

**Russell** Never believe what y'read in the papers, Sir. In any case, my relationship wi' Lysette is purely interlectual.

**Jackson** Sonja?

**Sonja** I don't think I'm feeling well, Sir.

**Tony** Don't say she's pregnant again.

**Sonja** *shoots up on to her feet* I never am. (*looks at the audience for a bit of sympathy*) My Gran says it's just a bit of wind.

**Mitchell** Sir, *I'd* like to get on with the lesson, so we can get it over with. I hate crowds.

**Celine** He wants to be a-l-o-n-e with you, Sir.

**Jackson** *warningly* Celine!

**Russell** *stands slowly as if about to make a speech* JackoSir ... It's out of order.

**Jackson** What's out of order?

**Russell** Not right – you teachin' us 'istory.

**Jackson** And why not?

**Russell** Well, you not bein' one of us. We're Brits. It's our 'istory. You lot 'ave yer own – slavery an' all that sort o' stuff, whereas our 'istory –

**Jackson** *provoked* Is all about kings and queens and glorious victories, is it?

**Denise** Mr. Jackson was at Oxford. He's a doctor.

**Tony** Then he can have a look at my ankle, it's really playing me up.

**Jackson** PhD actually, Denise. But thank you for pointing it out.

**Russell** Still, PH whatever it is you got, it isn't right. I mean, last week you were rantin' on about the Greatest Englishman – and we'd never even 'eard of 'im. So you called us ignorant.

**Jackson** I never use that word, Russ, you know that. Oh, and do sit down, this isn't the House of Commons.

**Russell** *sits* Well that's my point, Sir. I went past yer 'ouse o'Commons at the weekend. An' there were no statues to yer greatest Englishman. Only that bloke who kicked the crap out o' the Irish – Camelot –

**Jackson** Cromwell. Oliver Cromwell. Okay, it's true, Thomas Paine … (*he pauses, smiles with pride and a degree of relish*) Thomas Paine does not have a statue outside Parliament, and he is practically unknown in his native country. However, that ignorance is about to be put to rights – at least in this neck of the woods. You will soon be learning all about the great Tom Paine.

**Mitchell** I've had it up to here with history projects, Mr. Jackson. All that teamwork being supposed to be good for us – all this FOFO.

**Jackson** FOFO?

**Celine** *feigning surprise that* ***Mr. Jackson*** *is unaware of the expression* Oh, Sir – F-off and find out!

**Jackson** *amused* Good one, Celine. Just don't mention FOFO to the Headmaster.

**Tony** Is this Thomas Paine dead or alive, Sir? Because if he's dead, what's the point?

**Denise** He can be alive in spirit, can't he, Sir?

**Jackson** Thank you, Denise – exactly. This I promise you –

**Russell** Since when did teachers keep their promises?

**Jackson** I do, and I promise that learning about the ideas of Tom Paine might well change your lives.

**Sonja** A change of clothes'd do me. Our washin' machine blew up – shot my Gran right through a brick wall.

**Tony** What happened to her?

**Sonja** She had to do the washin' in the bath.

**Imran** She's lucky to have a bath. We've not had running water since Christmas.

**Celine** Sir, was Thomas Paine the one who had a glass eye and got his arm blowed off in Trafalgar Square?

**MITCHELL** That was Nelson, my hero. His last words were – 'Kiss me, Hardy!'

*A chorus of cheers, jeers and whistles from the class.*

**IMRAN** I was off, Sir, with my twisted fibula when you told us all this. So could you just recap on what this Thomas Hardy did to be our Greatest Englishman?

**JACKSON** Not Hardy – Paine. Tom Paine wrote books – they are his monument.

**DENISE** Mr. Jackson is writing a book about him, aren't you, Sir?

**RUSSELL** Who'll read it if it's in Swahili, Sir?

**JACKSON** Ah, Lysette.

***Lysette Thoma**s enters to wolf whistles from the males who stand and make gestures that might draw her attention to them. She ignores them.*

**MITCHELL** I told you she was having a boob job. Hello, Lysette?

**LYSETTE** You can shut up, Honeymoon.

*She goes to sit at the rear of the class but on an elevation so that she can be clearly seen by the audience.*

I'm in no mood for arsehole comments. (*pointing at **Russell***) And that applies to you in particular, Russell Morgan.

**JACKSON** Language, Lysette, please.

**RUSSELL** *stands. Looks at the audience, gestures as though in need of sympathy* Me? I didn't say nothin'.

**LYSETTE** Well before you do, shut it.

**IMRAN** It's her period, Sir. Women of all nations get like that.

**SONJA** Eskimos don't –

**LYSETTE** Sir – control this class.

**JACKSON** What's up, Lyse?

**LYSETTE** Lysette to you, Sir, or preferably Ms. Thomas. This place, that's what's up. (*she stands*) I'm being censored. For a start, our wonderful Headmaster, Mr. Lester, Hector the Spectre –

**JACKSON** Steady on, Lyse –

**LYSETTE** – won't allow us to change the name of the school magazine. It's got to go on being called 'Forward'. That's crap.

**JACKSON** Still, is 'StirCrap' such a good title?

**LYSETTE** The editorial team thinks so. And my article about this dump of a school is banned. He's not allowing one word of it to be printed. It'll cause *grave* offence, he says. Shit, that's what I want it to do.

**JACKSON** *warningly* Lysette!

**LYSETTE** Yes, Sir – bad language. It's a family trait, like irritable bowel syndrome.

*There is a pause.* ***Lysette*** *stares around the class. She sits, shaking her head.*

**RUSSELL** Old Thomas Paine would never 'ave put up wi' that, would 'e, Mr. JackoSir? Censorship, I mean.

**JACKSON** Leave Tom Paine out of this for the moment, will you?

**RUSSELL** Oh no, Sir – not if 'e's goin' to change our lives.

**TONY** *stands, offers a fist gesture in support* You show 'em, Lys – resign. (*sits*)

**MITCHELL** Who cares anyway? The only thing worth doing with the school mag is wipe your bum on it.

**LYSETTE** People will want to read 11C's section – I guarantee.

**IMRAN** At least there's our website.

**LYSETTE** Banned.

**SONJA** They can't –

**Lysette** Yes they can.

**Russell** Stuff 'em, then.

**Tony** I knew it'd never work, them asking us to do something special. We're the dunces in this school, the bread puddings; only when we get off our jacksies and act positive for once, look what happens.

**Jackson** Now listen! Listen ...(*there is quiet. Walks slowly up and down in front of the class*) Let's not jump to conclusions. (*stops, turns towards* ***Lysette***) What's Julian Hicks's position on all this, Lysette? After all, he's the editor.

**Lysette** *she gets up, less in a mood now, comes forward to what is her usual place. She glances imperiously at* ***Russell*** *who moves up to let her sit beside him* Don't mention his name in my presence. He's a prat and a creep.

**Mitchell** Julian – sounds tasty to me.

**Tony** His Dad's a politician and his Mum drives a BMW.

**Denise** He's very nice, actually. He speaks proper.

**Celine** That's why Miss Bolton fancies him. It's written all over her. Isn't that right, Mr. Jackson? – *you* must have noticed.

**Jackson** I certainly haven't. Now let's keep to the point – Julian's position on the proposed new title of the school mag, and Lysette's feature.

**Lysette** He hasn't got a position, other than sitting on the fence. Nice to me, nice to Mr. Lester.

**Tony** And very nice to Miss Bolton.

**Russell** What d'ya expect? They made Jules editor cos' e's one o' them.

**Denise** One of them?

**Russell** The people in charge, stupid.

**Tony** She's not stupid – just thick.

**DENISE** Shut up you.

**LYSETTE** Well Julian Hicks isn't the editor of 11C Section: that's ours. All we've got to express ourselves. Right, Mr. Jackson – or are you on the fence too?

**RUSSELL** JackoSir believes in free speech, don't you, Sir?

**JACKSON** I do. 102

**LYSETTE** Then you're with us – in our fight.

**TONY** *leaps to his feet* Fight? That's more like it. When does it start?

*Waits. They all wait.*

**LYSETTE** Mr. Jackson?

**JACKSON** Miss Thomas?

**RUSSELL** Doubtin' Thomas at the moment, JackoSir.

*There is an expectant silence.*

**TONY** Some fight. (*sits down, disappointed*)

**CELINE** Lys is asking, Sir – are you for us or against us?

**JACKSON** *he paces, pauses, surveys the class* Is it that easy?

**LYSETTE** *angry* That comment means you're not.

**IMRAN** Just what are we fighting about?

**MITCHELL** Free sex, I hope.

**TONY** Five poxy pages in a poxy school rag.

**LYSETTE** We're going to fight for justice. (*nodding*) The right to speak out, speak the truth, even if it causes (*mockingly*) *grave* offence. Just for once, why can't we be taken seriously? (*pause. She stands, makes room for herself, places her hands on her hips expectantly*) We are waiting, Mr. Jackson.

**JACKSON** Well ... I've not seen your article yet, but Miss Bolton –

she says it trashes the school.

**Lysette** It does. That's my right.

**Jackson** Unmercifully.

**Lysette** But there's not a word that isn't true.

**Denise** It's researched, Sir – all of it. We helped, didn't we, Lyse?

**Lysette** In a way, it's all our work, not just mine.

**Sonja** I like that bit about us bein' like a slave ship.

**Mitchell** It's sort of our chance, Sir.

**Celine** Yeah, for once to stop being the school joke.

*There is an expectant, vibrant silence.*

102 **Jackson** I'll see what I can do.

**Celine** *aping him* See what I can do … Big deal!

**Denise** That's not fair. Mr. Jackson sticks up for us.

**Russell** What about now?

**Lysette** *moves a step towards **Mr. Jackson**, stares at him defiantly* Okay Mr. Jackson, while you're making up your mind, seeing what you can do – I'm fighting. (*she looks round*) But I can't do it on my own. I'll be needing some help. Some solidarity.

**Mitchell** Russ has something solid he can offer you.

**Denise** That's disgusting.

**Lysette** Yes, well until this battle's won he can stick it up his jumper.

*Howls of laughter from the class.*

**Russell** At least I don't keep my brains in my tits. You've not an earthly. (*he stands, puts distance between himself and **Lysette** so that they seem to be on opposite sides of the argument*) The 'ole world'll kick y' in the what's-it, believe me. I mean, look at JackoSir: 'e spouts day an' night about Thomas Paine, the greatest ever Englishman, an' all that snot about 'uman rights, but what 'appens when the goin' gets rough? 'E does a nosedive at the first fence.

(*returns to his seat*)

Forget it, Lyse.

**Jackson** *irritated* I said – I'll do what I can. 102

**Tony** Still on probation, aren't you, Sir? – this being your first teaching job.

**Celine** I know what it's all about, this banning stuff. (*she stands, nodding vigorously*) The stiffs – our wonderful teachers – are wetting their pants because … Well, don't we all know? Come on, every-body – (*she gestures for the class to stand up*) Could it be…?

***Form 11C** bob up and down as they construct the answer to **Celine**'s question.*

**Mitchell** That 'orrible, ghastly, 'orrific – 89

**Tony** Gut-splattering –

**Imran** Knee-trembling –

**Sonja** Blood churdling –

**Celine** Come on everybody!

**Form 11C** *stand together, raise their arms and shout, in unison* INSPECTION! *(grinning, they lower their arms and stare expectantly at **Mr.Jackson**)*

**Jackson** Sit down, all of you. (*they sit. **Mr. Jackson** shakes his head*) Nothing to do with the Inspection.

**Lysette** Everything to do with the Inspection!

**Russell** I can 'ear it trickling down yer pants, JackoSir – ice-cold liquid terror!

**Tony** I like it! – liquid terror.

**Russell** An' it's spillin' all over the floor.

*The class stands again, almost threateningly. They nod and point at* ***Mr. Jackson****.*

Yeah, no wonder y'r shakin' in yer shoes, JackoSir. If 'alf of what Lyse says in 'er article is true – they'll shut the school down.

**Mitchell** Roll on the Inspection!

*The scene freezes, lights fade.*

## Scene 2

***Mr. Hector Lester****, Headmaster of the William Pitt School, is alone in his study. Behind him is a desk or table, and a chair. He is rehearsing a speech he will deliver at tomorrow's assembly. He addresses the audience from the front of the stage.*

**Lester** School! (*pauses. Stares imperiously around him*) Little by little ... Little by little? No, not positive enough. (*clears throat*) School! In recent Maths – months! We have made tremendous ... taken tremendous strides here at William Pitt. We have advanced up the league table of excellence with the rapidity of ... With impressive, nay, remarkable rapidity.

That position – our reputation in the community for educational excellence, let us not put too fine a point on it: top school in the district – is now, in the next few days, to be put to the test.

The Inspection –

*Knock at the door.* ***Mrs. Draper****, the School Secretary, enters.*

Yes, Mrs. Draper?

**Mrs Draper** Miss Bolton and Mr. Jackson to see you, Mr. Lester, as you requested.

***Lester*** *glances sideways as if into a mirror, explores his forehead with his fingers. He sighs.*

**LESTER** Do you think I'm losing hair, Mrs. Draper?

**MRS DRAPER** *hesitant* It's the stress of the job, Headmaster. The way things are going, you'll lose all your hair.

**LESTER** *brusquely* Thank you for those few kind words, Mrs. D. Now show them in, and make sure we are not disturbed.

**MRS DRAPER** Shall I serve coffee, Mr. Lester?

**LESTER** Coffee? Heavens no – they've already had their morning break.

*Enter* ***Miss Lorna Bolton*** *and* ***Jethro Jackson****.*

**LESTER** Good morning to you, colleagues. I'm grateful you could spare the time in your busy programmes – well, whatever.

Now Jesse –

**JACKSON** Jethro, Headmaster. Jesse was the unsuccessful presidential candidate for the United States some years ago.

**LESTER** And Laura, isn't it?

**MISS BOLTON** Lorna, Sir.

**LESTER** Of course. There's such a turnover of staff these days. Now sit down, sit down. (*they sit on two upright, uncomfortable chairs.* ***Lester*** *struts in front of them, then pauses, turns, stares hard at them*) We have a problem. Scores of problems, of course, but this one falls in to your, er, orbit. Indeed, Jesse –

**JACKSON** Jethro, Sir, or just plain Jeth.

**LESTER** Yes, yes. Between these four walls, Mr. Jackson, the problem is – how shall I put it? Something of your making.

**JACKSON** *My* making, Headmaster?

**LESTER** Permitting, nay, encouraging 11C of all groups in the school to have their own magazine, and even worse, their own website ... Good heavens, Jesse – they're hooligans. 102

**Jackson** Not all of them, Sir.

**Miss Bolton** It was my decision to give them a chance, Headmaster. And they do write some very, er, muscular poetry.

**Lester** Muscular – is that what you call it? 11C, Jesse –

**Jackson** Jethro, Sir –

**Lester** Are tomorrow's criminal fraternity. They're cut-throats, the lot of them. Bandits. I mean, Russell Morgan has been in court four times and it's not even a leap year.

**Jackson** True, but I've got hopes for the lad. Beneath all that bluster, there's a brain. And he's teamed up with Lysette Thomas on this thing.

**Lester** Well that's another mystery – what's a girl like that from a good family doing in 11C anyway? Miss Bolton?

**Miss Bolton** Lysette refuses to work, Headmaster. Everything we do here is pointless to her. However, she's suddenly discovered a talent.

**Jackson** She's a born journalist, Headmaster. I take it that's the problem you wish to discuss.

**Lester** Journalist, is that what you call her? Scurrilist, would be my description of her. She writes more scurrilous drivel than all the gutter press rolled into one.

**Jackson** Drivel, Sir? I wouldn't say –

**Lester** *aggressively* But I do say, Mr. Jackson. And so will the school governors, I assure you. One glance at Miss Thomas's article will have Lady Testard foaming at the mouth. Not to mention the girl's abominable spelling and the fact that she seems never to have heard of an apostrophe 's'. Don't you give them spelling and punctuation tests in English these days, Miss Bolton?

**Miss Bolton** Lysette's grammar and sentence structure, Headmaster, are very sound.

**Lester** *staring at her with incomprehension* The point I am making is not about grammar, or indeed spelling, Miss Bolton. It is about content. And Lady Testard –

**MISS BOLTON** But the magazine isn't written for Lady Testard, Sir.

**LESTER** Miss Bolton, mercifully you do not have to deal with our Chair of Governors. (*he pauses. He paces. He glances at the two of them, shaking his head as if continuing a conversation with himself*) And the problem, colleagues – the crisis! – should be staring you both in the face. (*pauses*) The Inspection! Our future depends on a good report and yet here she is, this slip of a girl, scarcely out of nappies –

**JACKSON** Quite mature for her age, actually, Headmaster –

**MISS BOLTON** Very bright.

**LESTER** Bright? – dynamite! Producing... (*he seizes from his desk a photocopy of Lysette's article. Waves it in the air*) ... an undercover story that threatens to blow the lid off everything.

According to Miss Lysette Thomas, gifted journalist, this school, my school, your school – is the drugs centre of the city. (*pauses, stares at **Mr. Jackson** and **Miss Bolton***) For protection racketeering, the school has no equal this side of Chicago. We're infested with Chinese Triads and West Indian Yardies who have the run of the premises.

**MISS BOLTON** She did her research, Sir.

**LESTER** Soliciting rumour and hearsay, you mean. And that's just for starters. The entire staff is accused of fixing results to boost our position in the leagues tables. This whippersnapper is accusing us of being guilty of fraud – criminals!

*Silence. **Mr. Lester** stares at his staff.*

Well?

**JACKSON** She stands by what's she's written, Headmaster.

**LESTER** Are you suggesting that one jot or tittle, one milligram, one hundredth of one percent is true?

**JACKSON** I'm not sure about that bit on the Triads, Sir. Students tend to think that all Chinese are members.

**LESTER** *aghast* So the rest you think is true?

***Jackson** looks at **Miss Bolton**.*

**Miss Bolton** It's, somewhat exaggerated in places, Head –

**Lester** *yelling* Somewhat exaggerated?

**Miss Bolton** Lysette is a very bitter girl. And to be perfectly honest with you, Sir, our results do seem to be a trifle – on the high side, considering –

**Lester** I don't want to hear any more. Not a word! *(he slumps into his chair, leans forward on to his desk and drops his head into his hands. Slowly he raises his eyes, then his head)* Only the other day, Lady Testard – you know what contacts she has with ministers and such people? – she was saying, in strictest confidence, mind, that in *her* opinion, half the staff don't deserve paying in tap washers. (*he stands, weary*) In short, we are already perched on the edge of a precipice. Catastrophe is just around the corner. If this article sees the light of day, we will become the laughing-stock of the educational world.

**Jackson** However, Headmaster, it would show that we are fulfilling the government's primary aims of education – nurturing independence –

**Miss Bolton** Creativity –

**Jackson** Problem-solving –

**Miss Bolton** And teamwork.

**Lester** Poppycock! (*he stands*) Such aims may be admirable. But it is not what the system is about.

**Jackson** So what is it about, Headmaster?

**Lester** The good of the school – that's what it's about. And in that regard, the two of you have singularly failed to persuade Miss Thomas that it is in the best interests of the school as well as her own best interests, to consign this piece of trash to the waste bin.

**Miss Bolton** Sir, I did suggest, er – modifications to the article.

**Lester** Modifications! Good grief, it's all got to go.

**Miss Bolton** In fact, I did write a version – one that is less – er –

**Jackson** Explosive.

**Miss Bolton** Yes, that might pass muster with you, with the governors.

**Lester** And Miss Thomas's response?

**Miss Bolton** No luck, Sir. They're not her words. And to be honest, her piece is much more lively.

**Lester** More lively, is it? (*he stands*) Well this is what I think of it. (*he rips it up. He reaches for a waste paper basket and stuffs the offending article into it*) Don't worry. I have kept a photocopy for Lady Testard. Now, Miss Bolton, I want your version – and only your version – on my desk by the end of the day. (*he sits*)

**Miss Bolton** Lysette won't ever trust me again, Sir.

**Lester** *leans forward threateningly* And nor will I, Miss Bolton.

*Enter* ***Mrs. Draper****.*

**Mrs. Draper** Sorry to disturb you, Headmaster. But there is a Mr. Paine to see you. He hasn't an appointment, but he insists it is a matter of urgency.

*There is a flickering of the stage lights as if to indicate that at this point reality itself is also on the edge.*

**Lester** We really must get the wiring fixed in this place. (*pause*) Paine?

**Mrs Draper** Yes, he is quite oddly dressed, Sir; and wearing a wig.

**Lester** A wig?

**Mrs Draper** In fact he looks as though he's just stepped out of a Jane Austen novel. (*she chuckles*) Quite charming.

***Mr. Lester*** *has frozen. He stares into space.*

And buckles on his shoes, Sir.

**Lester** *in panic. He is up, pacing* I knew it – knew it! (*he stares ferociously yet fearfully at **Miss Bolton** and **Mr. Jackson***) You know what is happening beneath our very noses? Huh? – the Inspection has already begun. That's what they do these days. They tell you one date and then come three weeks early. (*with a sense of horror*) In disguise! Anything to throw us off the scent.

**Mrs Draper** That'll be it, then, Headmaster, because Mr. Paine expressed a particular wish to talk to Form 11C.

**Lester** Talk to 11C? Oh my God – we're doomed!

*Scene freezes, lights fade.*

## Scene 3

*The playing field at William Pitt School slopes upwards steeply to a knoll on which there was once an ancient fortification. All that is left are the remains of the gatehouse. If there is to be scenery then there should be the remnants of an arched doorway; if a simulation is to be created with the stage boxes then these can be haphazardly stacked, with one of the large step-ladders forming an arch.*

*The location is a meeting place for students and is referred to as Fort Pox.*

*Close to the front of the stage, **Julian Hicks**, prefect and editor of the school magazine, 'Forward', is surrounded by members of **11C**. He should be standing on a box somewhat higher than the rest so that the audience gets a clear view of him.*

**Julian Hicks** No, I am not – not, not, not – in favour of censorship.

**Lysette** Then why've you brought us out here in secret?

**Julian** Because this spot's the only place we can talk about things frankly.

**Tony** If the school's bugged, why isn't this old ruin? After all, it's here all the mischief happens.

**Celine** Shut up about sex, Tony. Is the school really bugged, Julian?

**JULIAN** It could be. All I'm arguing –

**RUSSELL** Delayin' Lyse's article till the Inspection's over is censorship in my book.

**JULIAN** Do we want to get the school a bad name?

**MITCHELL** Who cares?

**SONJA** When you get a bad name, it sticks.

**IMRAN** You'll know all about that, then, Sonja.

**SONJA** You should wash your mouth out, Im-ran – and go back to Calcutta where you belong.

**IMRAN** I belong in Penge, actually.

**CELINE** It's draughty out here.

**TONY** You shouldn't wear such a short skirt.

**JULIAN** Can we keep to the point?

**DENISE** This place gives me the creeps. I keep thinking somebody's going to come out from that arch and hit me with a knobkerrie.

**MITCHELL** Ball an' chain more like.

**JULIAN** What I'd like us all to think about is priorities. I mean, we have to think of our futures. Not just exams, but references, that kind of thing. The way things are these days, one dodgy reference can follow you around for ever.

**MITCHELL** Yeah, they've got everythin' about us on computer. If we fart in class, it's on the computer.

**RUSSELL** Not to mention the cameras. Eyin' us up every which way. In the bogs, down every corridor, round every bleedin' corner. Spies. We should destroy 'em. In the name of privacy.

**TONY** What, so you can pinch the school trophies – again?

**DENISE** The cameras're supposed to be for our protection.

**RUSSELL** Don't matter – we've a right not to be spied on.

**JULIAN** Okay. Perhaps we could do a piece for the mag on all this surveillance.

**MITCHELL** What's that in plain English?

**JULIAN** Watching us.

**TONY** Do they watch us when we're having a crap or working ourselves off?

**DENISE** We're not as disgusting as him, Julian.

**JULIAN** I think you sympathise with my point, Denise.

**DENISE** Call me Den.

**MITCHELL** It's your point she's after, Jules.

**LYSETTE** I'm not buying this – an article on surveillance, on spying, in exchange for banning 'Pitt School is Pants!'?

**RUSSELL** Great title, Lyse.

**JULIAN** Not banning, Lysette. Rescheduling it.

**RUSSELL** Are we speakin' the same language?

**LYSETTE** Words, Julian. The action's the same. Postponement's as bad as banning.

**RUSSELL** Who's bin gettin' at you, Jules?

**MITCHELL** Miss Bolton, right, Julie? Leary Lorna. She strips you naked every time she sets eyes on you.

**CELINE** I'm not sure I blame her.

**JULIAN** Thank you, Celine.

**TONY** What's it matter anyway? Let's just take a vote and then bog off.

**LYSETTE** *hotly. She takes her place on a 'soapbox' beside* ***Julian*** It matters. Don't you all see? If this thing doesn't matter, nothing else does. If we're not free to speak the truth, then why are we here? Stuck five days a week in this dump. Forced to listen to niggling nerds who tremble at the very word 'inspection'.

**TONY** Niggling nerds – I like it!

**LYSETTE** Sad cases, most of them, who teach us to be nice, conform, take our place in the queue of life –

**CELINE** Queue of life! Lyse, you ought to be on TV.

**LYSETTE** Educating us – yeah? Some hopes, except to teach us never to step out of line so that one day somebody can sit on us and all we'll be capable of doing is squeaking – even if we can remember to do that. It matters!

*Applause and cheers from the group.*

**RUSSELL** Good on you, Lyse. I wish I'd said that myself.

**SONJA** Shush, Russ –

**IMRAN** We're not alone...

*There is a sudden, complete silence, except for a wind that whistles, hauntingly, through the stone arch. The actors all turn to face the arch behind them. This is now illuminated and the foreground is cast into shadow.*

**RUSSELL** What's up?

**TONY** *in shock* We have a visitor.

*Framed within the arch is a figure, strangely dressed, in a wig.*

**DENISE** I knew this place was haunted.

*The visitor is* ***Mr. Thomas Paine****. A spotlight illuminates him and follows him as he steps forward into the 21st century.*

**TOM PAINE** *brightly* Form 11C?

**RUSSELL** That's us. Who're you?

**PAINE** Good morning. I'm delighted to meet you. (*he approaches the group which opens up for him. He remains in the spotlight, 11C in its periphery*) My name is Thomas Paine. My friends – and a few of my enemies – call me Tom.

**Sonja** *almost to herself* He's in fancy dress.

**Russell** Not ... *the* Tom Paine?

*We hear the wind again through the stone arch.*

**Julian** This isn't happening.

**Lysette** *almost triumphantly* Oh yes it is! (*she steps towards **Tom**, holding out her hand*)

**Lysette** Welcome to the twenty-first century, Mr. Paine! (*she gazes around at the rest of 11C*) You couldn't have come at a better time.

*The scene freezes into a tableau as **Lysette** and **Tom Paine** shake hands. The light slowly fades but the haunting wind continues for a few moments.*

**Sonja** *her voice emerging from total darkness* But Tom Paine's dead... isn't he?

## Scene 4

*Back in the Headmaster's study. **Mr. Lester** is at his desk. **Miss Bolton** and **Mr. Jackson** are about to depart. **Mrs. Draper** is at the door.*

**Lester** No, don't leave for the moment. I want you to share with me the horror of what schools inspection teams get up to these days, in order to worm their way into our trousers – sorry, secrets.

Mrs. Draper, you may show Mr. – er – Paine in now, thank you.

**Mrs Draper** Oh, he's gone off, Sir.

**Lester** Gone off?

**Mrs Draper** With 11C.

**Lester** Impossible!

**Mrs Draper** No, they'll all be up at the ruin. Funny old sort, he is. Very eloquent – a real way with words; though I think he must have a bit of a weakness for the bottle – he's got a very red nose.

**Jackson** *mystified* Does he – spell his name with an 'e', Mrs. Draper?

**Mrs. Draper** He didn't spell it out for me, but his first name's Thomas, though his friends and some of his enemies call him Tom.

*She moves off stage.*

**Lester** Enemies – he'll have enemies all right. I'm surprised inspectors haven't been murdered before now. Did you give him permission, Jesse, to take 11C out of class?

**Miss Bolton** Actually, it's my class, Headmaster.

**Lester** Then why aren't you teaching them?

**Miss Bolton** Well I'm here, aren't I, Sir?

**Lester** Get them back. This instant. God knows what they could be telling him.

**Jackson** Is that wise, Headmaster?

**Lester** Back, I want them back.

**Miss Bolton** Wouldn't it look as though we've something to hide?

**Lester** Haven't we?

**Jackson** No more than –

**Lester** *calls* Mrs. Draper? I want you to press the fire alarm.

**Mrs Draper** *reappears* Fire alarm, Sir?

**Lester** Don't keep repeating what I say, woman – sound the fire alarm at once.

**Mrs Draper** But Headmaster, the fire brigade says –

**Lester** Damn what the fire brigade says – sound the alarm!

*Shrill, prolonged burst from the fire alarm.*

## Scene 5

*In Form 11C's classroom.* ***Mr. Jackson*** *is back with his class register.*

**TONY** What was the point of that, Sir?

**JACKSON** Fire practice makes perfect. Now there are two missing: Russell and Lysette. Anyone seen them?

**CELINE** They went with that bloke.

**JACKSON** Which bloke?

**DENISE** Your friend, Mr. Jackson.

**TONY** The greatest Englishman – Mr. Thomas Paine, Tom to his friends –

**IMRAN** And some of his enemies.

**JACKSON** Well for your enlightenment, the Headmaster is convinced he is a schools inspector.

**MITCHELL** I get it, in disguise, wanting us to bad-mouth the school.

**JACKSON** That's what Mr. Lester fears –

**DENISE** It was nothing like that, Sir.

**SONJA** I liked him, even though he had a red nose –

**CELINE** He just asked about –

**IMRAN** Slavery.

**JACKSON** Slavery?

**TONY** Yeah, whether we'd abolished it or not – weird!

**SONJA** Lyse said we hadn't, abolished it, that is.

**IMRAN** We're still slaves, she said.

**DENISE** Especially us women.

**JACKSON** So I suppose he talked to you about the rights of man?

**DENISE** And women.

**Jackson** Very strange. If he is an inspector, it's a clever disguise.

**Tony** He's no inspector, Mr. Jackson. He's the real thing.

*The class is silent. We hear again the rush of the wind through the stone arch.*

**Jackson** *impressed, his thoughts in turmoil* Did he say anything else?

**Mitchell** He wanted to know if women had got the vote yet.

**Jackson** And what did Lysette have to say about that?

**Celine** Yeah, we got the vote, but that's all we've got.

**Denise** What's Saudi Arabia, Sir?

**Jackson** A country in the middle east.

**Denise** Well Lyse went on about women out there. No votes. An' they're forced to wear pack-a-macks over their faces.

**Jackson** Yashmaks.

**Sonja** What are them, Sir?

**Jackson** A sort of veil – covers the face except for the eyes.

**Denise** That's not fair.

**Celine** An' they're not allowed to be educated proper, like what we are.

**Imran** Mr. Paine was shocked.

**Tony** As I say, JackoSir – he didn't look like an inspector to me. He was like a … ghost.

**Celine** I don't believe in ghosts, but I believe in life after death. Otherwise, what's the point?

**Sonja** My Grandad came back from the dead once. But we were all out at the pub.

**Jackson** Before we get on to the meaning of life, death and resurrection, let me just get this clear. Russell and Lysette stayed with, ah – Mr. Paine?

*Pause.*

**Mitchell** They went with him, sort of.

**Jackson** With him – where?

**Denise** Through the archway.

**Jackson** Archway?

**Mitchell** At Fort Pox, Sir.

**Jackson** But there's no archway, just a lot of old rubble.

**Imran** It was there all right. Straight through, they went.

**Tony** I said he was a ghost.

**Denise** He invited us all to go. Then the fire alarm went.

*There is a long pause.*

**Celine** Oh my God, they could have disappeared.

**Sonja** Or been abdicted –

**Jackson** Abducted. (*in shock*) I think … I'd better have another word with the Headmaster.

*Again, wind through the archway.*

He's right. We do have a problem.

## Scene 6

*The scene switches to the TV studio of Channel 99 as the 3500th edition of* This Was Your Life *begins. The boxes and benches used for Form 11C's classroom have been rearranged to make two or three tiers. The studio audience, chiefly made up of* ***Form 11C****, is seated on the tiers, facing the real audience, and in shadow.*

*Also, as members of the stage audience are the following:* ***Voices 1*** *and* ***2****,* ***Julius Caesar****,* ***Henry VIII****,* ***Mrs. Burke****, wife of* ***Edmund Burke*** *the great personal enemy of* ***Tom Paine****, an* ***Angel*** *and* ***President George Washington****.*

***Miss Bolton****,* ***Mr. Lester*** *and* ***Julian Hicks*** *also appear.*

*In front are a couple of cameras on tripods – purely as indicators that this is a TV studio – and a spotlight draws a white circle on the stage floor.*

*As appropriate music is played, there is applause from the studio audience. The well-known presenter* ***Jeth Jackson*** *steps into the spotlight and the applause reaches a crescendo.*

**JACKSON** *to the audience, and more like a circus ringmaster than a TV presenter* Welcome – welcome, welcome, welcome to TV Channel 99 and its totally, oatally favourite programme, 'This Was Your Life – In the Hot Seat'. I promise you it's going to be a Gas Mark Ten baking night tonight.

*The spotlight sweeps swiftly across stage to focus on* ***Lysette****,* ***Russell*** *and* ***Tom Paine****.*

**RUSSELL** There isn't no Channel 99.

**LYSETTE** You didn't say you were bringing us to a TV show, Mr. Paine.

**PAINE** Tom, please. Only my enemies call me Mister. And some, like Mr. Burke, do not even call me that.

**RUSSELL** Burke? Didn't 'e play for West'am?

**PAINE** To be honest, I'm as surprised as you are to be here. Am I being tried?

*Spotlight reverts to* ***Jeth Jackson****.*

**JACKSON** I am proud, ladies and gentlemen, particularly proud, to be introducing you this evening to one of England's greatest – nay *the* greatest Englishman; a man who has long been one of my heroes.

*Applause.*

**VOICE 1** *on the back row of the studio audience, picked out by the spotlight* Lord Wellington – it's gotta be! Knocked the stuffin' out o' the Frenchies.

**VOICE 2** *On the front row of the studio audience, again picked out by the spotlight* Winston Churchill gets my vote. He knocked the stuffin' out o' the Jerries.

**VOICE 1** *spotlight* Aye, 'e was the best England manager the team ever 'ad.

**VOICE 2** *spotlight* That was Alf Ramsey, surely.

**JACKSON** *spotlight* No, not your fighting men, nor your cynical statesman or plotting politician – though politics was his life.

**VOICE 1** *spotlight* Politics? – b-o-rin'!

**VOICE 2** *spotlight* A bit o'skirt wouldn't come amiss.

*Now the full stage lights illuminate the studio audience.*

**TONY** Hey, Russ, Lyse – so this is where you got to!

***Lysette*** *and* ***Russell*** *come forward.*

**LYSETTE** Oh lord, the whole of 11C's arrived.

*The others budge up for the newcomers.*

**DENISE** I've always wanted to be on TV.

**CELI NE** I was on Top of the Pops once.

**Mitchell** Yeah, we found a talent scout in your knickers the following morning.

**Sonja** Doesn't Mr. Jackson look gorgeous?

*The stage lights dim and the spotlight returns to centre on* ***Jeth Jackson****.*

**Jackson** It is not a word of exaggeration to say, Ladies and 102
Gentlemen, folks at home – that this is an historical moment. For here with us this evening is a man who created not one, but two revolutions in his lifetime, in two continents – and gave us a most wonderful gift…

**Voice 1** *unimpressed* Like what?

**Jackson** Democracy!

**Voice 2** Some gift. Ninety percent of folks in this country couldn't even spell it.

**Jackson** Before I name our distinguished guest, and present him with his Book of Everlasting Fame and Honour, just a reminder – as this is our 3500th edition – of some of the prestigious celebrities who have appeared on 'This Was Your Life'. Ladies and gentlemen – Mr. Julius Caesar!

*Cheers.*

**Julius Caesar** *spotlight picks him out at the back of the studio audience. He stands, in a white toga covered in 'blood' marks* I'm not talking to you, Jackson.

**Jackson** No? Why ever not, O Caesar?

**Caesar** You assured me there'd be no mention of burning down the great library at Alexandria, particularly as it was an accident.

**Jackson** Three million precious manuscripts destroyed, practically the entire knowledge of the ancient world, and it was an accident?

**Caesar** I just torched a few ships in the harbour. How was I to know the fire would spread and that parchment was so combustible? I mean, fair do's – wasn't I the first to open a free library for the rabble?

**Denise** Rabble? He's talking about us, I think.

**Jackson** Sorry, Caesar, we had to edit that bit out – lack of time, I'm afraid.

**Caesar** That's not all. I object to you bringing on to the programme my assassins, my murderers, slimy Cassius in particular – I call that really bad taste.

**Jackson** Oh but my assistant, the Lovely Lorna – she…

*Cheers for **Lorna Bolton** as she steps into **Jackson's** spotlight.*

**Tony** – should wear short skirts more often.

**Miss Bolton** I assure you, O Caesar, we confiscated all their knives at the door.

**Caesar** Then how come I ended up full of holes?

**Miss Bolton** It was Brutus, Sir, he'd hidden a Stanley knife down his stocking.

**Caesar** Well that's the last time I do you Brits a favour.

**Voice 1** Ged 'im off!

***Caesar** fades.*

**Jackson** Now a big hand, folks, for one of the nation's favourites – King Henry the Eighth!

*Applause and cheers.*

**Henry** *standing and in spotlight* You're a bounder, Sir – confronting me with all seven of my wives at once.

**Jackson** Not to mention Mr. William Tyndale, who you burnt at the stake for printing the Bible in English.

**Lysette** Banning by burning – makes you shudder, doesn't it?

**Russell** I thought you only 'ad six wives, Fatso.

**Henry** Don't believe what you read in the history books, kid.

**Russell** Frankly, I don't believe in nothin'. Not God, not 'eroes –

**Celine** How about the Dead Sea Scrawls?

**Jackson** *fleetingly as teacher* Scrolls, Celine.

**Russell** Not philosophers, not kings and queens –

**Mitchell** Queens are my favourite!

**Henry** Mine too. I just couldn't get enough of 'em.

**Russell** Not democracy – not nothin'.

**Lysette** Rubbish, Russell. You believe in what's right.

**Russell** Do I?

**Jackson** *swiftly* What's right … tremendous, as our England football manager used to say before they brought in a foreigner who could speak English proper –

**Miss Bolton** *flouncing* Proper*ly*, I think, Jethro.

**Jackson** Thank you, Lorna, Babe. Yes – what's *right*, which brings us to tonight's guest, a giant among writers –

**Voice 1** Oh no, not one o'them!

**Jackson** The father of human rights, in this country – in all countries – Mr. Thomas Paine! 102

***Tom Paine** raises a hand to protect his eyes from the glare of the spotlight. **Lysette** leads him to centre stage.*

**Lysette** *in wonder as though the name has not registered yet* Tom Paine!

**Form 11C** *together* Yeah!

**Voice 2** Tom who? Never 'eard of 'im.

**Lysette** *sharply, impatiently* Well you will now.

**Voice 1** An' if 'e don't?

**Lysette** Form 11C'll make him.

**Mitchell** Ease up, Lyse – that's censorship.

**Lysette** On the contrary, deliberate ignorance is censorship.

**Jackson** *reading from a leather-bound volume* Born in Thaxted in the county of Essex in 1737 to a Quaker family.

**Sonja** They say Quaker oats are good for your skin.

**Jackson** Incidentally, is it true to say, Mr. Paine? –

**Paine** Tom, please.

**Jackson** – Tom, that late in your life, when you asked that you should be buried in Quaker ground, they turned you down?

**Paine** On account of my views on religion, I guess; or rather the institutions of religions.

**Jackson** You loved God but hated the church?

***Tom** now turns towards the audience. The spotlight is on him and remains on him as **Jackson** reads the details of his life.*

*If it is possible, and a screen is available, slides could be projected: portraits of Paine and details as they are referred to, such as a photograph of the White Hart Inn in Lewes, the covers of Paine's books etc.*

**Paine** Tell me a church, a religion, that has not got blood of the innocent on its hands.

**Jackson** You became, as a youth, a staymaker.

**Russell** What's that when we're at 'ome?

**Lysette** Women's corsets. They made fat women look thin.

**Tony** Bring back corsets, I say!

**Celine** You would say that – but it's not fair on fat women.

**Jackson** Later, in the town of Lewes in Sussex, you became a customs officer, collecting taxes on behalf of the Crown. There, you joined a debating society that met at the White Hart Inn.

**Paine** *warming to the details of his own past* Yes, the Headstrong Club as I remember. It was there that my views on society began to develop.

**Jackson** A friend of yours, Mr. William Lee, was so impressed by you that he wrote you a poem. We have been unable to locate Mr. Lee, so the Lovely Lorna will oblige.

*Briefly the lights dim and a spotlight centres on* ***Miss Bolton****.*

**Miss Bolton** *reciting*

Immortal PAINE...
Thy logic vanquish'd error and thy mind
No bounds but right and truth confined –

*Normal lighting resumes.*

**Lysette** I like that: no bounds but those of Truth and Right. We'll print it in 'StirCrap', Tom.

**Jackson** *inspired* The poem concludes –

Thy soul of fire must sure ascend the sky.

**Tony** Soul of fire – wonderful.

**Lysette** At last we're hearing something worth listening to, Mr. Jackson.

**Jackson** Didn't I tell you? – the greatest Englishman!

**Henry** Nobody wrote poems like that about Henry the Eighth.

**Paine** Because you, like all monarchs, Flash Harry, took life rather than gave it; a parasite on the back of the common people.

**Henry** *stands, stomps forward* How dare you, Sir? Are you forgetting all the films I've starred in, all the TV series? Just how many movies have *you* been in, y'red-nosed rebel? Huh, I've better things to do with my time than stay here and be insulted.

*He marches across stage.*

**Tony** Such as what?

**Henry** *pauses, turns* Guest appearance in 'Coronation Street' – that's what!

*He strides off.*

**Imran** Good riddance!

**Henry** *shouting from off stage* I heard that!

**Russell** Y'should see the Royals today, Tom.

**Paine** That shocks me, lad. *(**Tom** turns to the audience, holds out his hands as if he simply cannot believe what he has been told)* Don't say England isn't a republic yet?

**Lysette** We're still in chains, Tom.

**Jackson** In your book 'Common Sense', Tom, you wrote, 'Freedom hath been hunted round the globe' –

**Paine** *turns towards **Jackson**, but remains with the audience half in view* Yes, and 'England hath given freedom warning to depart'.

**Russell** Oh we're free all right – to decide whether we want a Big Mac or a Kingburger.

**Sonja** My Gran's got free teeth, only she lost 'em down the lav.

**Tony** Hey, look what the cat's brought in – Old Lester the Jester. Evenin', Headmaster.

***Lester** enters, seemingly oblivious to his surroundings.*

**Lester** Sit down, everyone.

*The class stand up, salute, then sit down.*

*To **Tony*** You, boy, will report to me at four o'clock prompt. And that goes for the rest of you hooligans from Form 11C.

**Celine** Can't you see, Sir – we're on telly!

**Lester** What is all this nonsense, Jesse? And Miss Bolton, didn't I warn you about split skirts and low necklines, especially with the Inspection coming on?

**Miss Bolton** We're going out live, Sir.

**Jackson** Ladies and gentlemen, if we could just –

**Lester** Television? Rubbish. This is just another of those stupid computer games making us think it's all happening when it isn't.

**Imran** It's called virtual reality, Sir.

**Mitchell** Beats real life every time.

**Lester** You are being deceived – all of you. This Mr. Paine is an imposter, being in reality a schools inspector in disguise. But he didn't fool me for an instant. I've already written to the Deputy Prime Minister on the matter.

**Celine** Sit down, Sir – you're spoilin' the show.

*__Miss Bolton__ provides __Lester__ with a chair at the side of the studio audience and coaxes him to sit. Briefly she smoothes his hair from behind.*

**Miss Bolton** You are definitely thinning on top, Headmaster.

**Jackson** Which brings us, folks, to our next witness – Sir Julian Hicks, who has generously granted us 60 seconds of his time.

*Enter __Julian Hicks__, somewhat greyer than in his school days.*

**Celine** That's Jules!

**Sonja** *Stands, steps forward* Hey, Julian, it's us – 11C.

**Julian** Thank you, but my private secretary will deal with your enquiries.

**Russell** *stands* Come off it, Jules, it's your old playmates.

**Julian** *ignoring his past* Sorry, I'm a very busy man.

*__Sonja__ sits, disappointed. __Russell__ shrugs and sits.*

**Julian** As for Mr. Lester's complaint, I have made exhaustive enquiries. No inspector of the name Thomas Paine is known to us –

**Lysette** Toffee-nosed sod.

**Paine** Another disguise, I perceive. *(he points to **Sir Julian**)* Mr. Edmund Burke – no other. Long time no see, Eddy.

**Julian** I beg your pardon?

**Jackson** Yes, Mr. Burke, your mortal enemy, Tom, who condemned the French Revolution, poured scorn upon the principles you advocated, of equality and the rights of the common man, and referred to the people as a swinish multitude –

**Julian** I never did. Even if it were true, it would be politically incorrect to do so –

*Enter **Mrs. Edmund Burke**, preferably in voluminous turn-of-the-19th century dress. She gives **Julian** a hearty push.*

**Mrs. Burke** Oh move over, Jules, you nancy.

*She addresses the audience.*

**Mrs. Burke** I'm *Mrs.* Burke, you poor ignorant rabble, and I'm 'ere to defend my 'usband Eddy who's gone to the palace to receive 'is bribe – oops, stipend – of £1500 from 'is majesty King George. *(taking the audience into her confidence, lowering her voice a little)* An' well 'e deserves it, brown-nosin' 'as 'e 'as to do wi' Royalty. *(she turns, points accusingly at **Tom Paine**)* You, Mr. Tom Red Nose Paine, deserve an 'orsewhip across yer Jerusalem for what you writ about my 'ubby's book, the title of which 'as too many silly-bulls for me to remember.

**Jackson** 'Reflections on the Revolution in France –

**Miss Bolton** and on the Proceedings in Certain Societies in London –

**Jackson** relative to that event'.

**Mrs. Burke** Somethin' like that. Not my kind o' bedtime readin'.

**Julian** *facing one of the cameras* We have, as ministers entrusted with public responsibility, to look at all issues with care, consider both sides, strike a balance.

***Mr. Lester** has risen from his chair and crosses to **Mrs. Burke**. He grasps her, holds her at arm's length and displays her to the studio audience and the audience itself.*

**Mrs. Burke** 'Ere, who're y'maulin'?

**Lester** Another imposter, Jesse. Mr. Burke was a man of rare learning and distinction, a philosopher, so how could his wife have dropped her h's so lamentably?

**Mrs. Burke** They couldn't get nobody else to play this part. So get yer 'ands off me or I'll have you charged with egregious molestation.

**Jackson** Tom, your own great book, 'The Rights of Man', was an eloquent and –

**Mrs. Burke** An' vicious –

**Jackson** Answer to the anti-democratic sentiments expressed by Mr. Burke.

**Mrs. Burke** Pen full o'poison!

**Jackson** You called Mr. Burke's tome on the French Revolution –

**Paine** Yes, 'a pathless wilderness of rhapsodies'.

**Tony** Pathless wilderness – great!

**Lysette** I like that! Go on, Tom.

**Imran** You'd think he was talking about today.

**Jackson** ***proudly*** From 'The Rights of Man', Volume 1, 1791.

*There is a moment of silence; we hear the haunting wind again. The spotlight falls on **Lysette**.*

**LYSETTE** *speaking as though in a dream* 'The Rights of Man'. How sweet that sounds!

*The full lights return.*

And what do we get at William Pitt School? With this stupid inspection coming on, we get a pathless wilderness – but without the rhapsody.

**TONY** Like it!

**MITCHELL** I appreciate a bit of rhapsody, specially on a Saturday night.

**LESTER** You've no right to say such things, Lysette Thomas!

**LYSETTE** And you've no right to tell me I've no right, Hector Lester!

**JACKSON** Listen, both of you!

**PAINE** I wrote about the unity of man.

**CELINE** I hope that includes us women.

**PAINE** Of course, Celine.

**CELINE** That's nice, he remembers my name. Mr. Lester doesn't. And Sir Julian's forgot it.

**IMRAN** Do those rights apply to aliens like me, Tom? I mean, that's what they call us Pakis – swines, yet we don't even eat pigs!

**PAINE** Men are all of one degree. I stand by that. They are born equal.

**SONJA** I wasn't. I was left on a doorstep.

**MITCHELL** Me, I was born queer, not equal.

**JACKSON** *enthusiastically* You wrote, Tom –

**PAINE** It is wrong to say God made rich and poor; He made only male and female, and He gave them the earth for their inheritance.

**CELINE** My Mum inherited haemorrhoids. They can't 'alf be painful.

**Jackson** In your writings, Tom, you attacked slavery, the conquest of India, you argued for old age pensions, public education, social security –

**Voice 1** Then how come none of us 'as ever 'eard of 'im?

**Tony** Cos 'e slagged off the Royals, that's why.

**Mitchell** An'all them other fat cats –

**Voice 2** Hey, Jeth, this is gettin' borin' – what about the scandals?

**Voice 1** Me, I think I preferred the programme on Adolf Hitler.

**Voice 2** Oh no, I can't go along with you there. Old Adolf spent the entire programme spoutin' on about cheatin' referees in the World Cup.

**Russell** Shut it, will you? Or you'll be sharin' a knuckle-sarny wi' Adolf.

**Denise** Oh, Mr. Jackson – this is your best history project ever.

**Imran** A lot better than doing the Dead Sea Squalls.

**Jackson** *as teacher* Scrolls, Imran, not squalls.

**Russell** I never thought I'd say this, but for the first time in my life I've bin 'earin' somethin' worth list'nin' to. Tom – to be equal, you gotta be free, right?

**Lysette** Cool! I wish I'd said that, Russ.

**Russell** An' that's the first time y'ever called me Russ.

**Lysette** It's the first time you deserved it.

**Paine** Freedom, Russ – yes. The first and foremost human right.

**Julian** Believe me, everyone, there are no votes in human rights. Absolutely none. People think with their pockets.

**Denise** And who made us that way?

**Julian** It has to be recognised that school league tables –

**Lysette** Don't do anything for equality.

**VOICE 1** Is this a party political broadcast or can we all join in?

**JULIAN** As I was saying, before being interrupted –

**LYSETTE** Shut up!

**JULIAN** Ah, so you are in favour of freedom of speech, Miss Thomas, only when it suits you?

**TONY** He's got a point, Lys.

**JACKSON** Tom, a word from you?

**PAINE** Very well. *(clears throat)* Whether in heaven or hell, or in whatever state man –

**SONJA** And woman –

**PAINE** Thank you, Sonja … whatever state man – or woman – be supposed to exist in hereafter, the good and the bad are the only distinctions.

**TONY** The good and the bad are the only distinctions: I'll have to think about that.

**CELINE** Then me and Sir Jules here is no different.

**LYSETTE** Tom was talking about what ought to be, not what is.

**LESTER** There you go, muddying the waters. School inspections are about excellence not equality. And another thing, Mr. Paine – where in the National Curriculum does your so-called mighty work, 'The Rights of Man' appear? In History, Geography, Biology, Physics?

**MRS BURKE** I'd 'ave thought it was obvious, 'eadmaster. It doesn't appear because it's, it's … come on now, Sir Julie, Baby, what's the word?

**JULIAN** Subversive?

**RUSSELL** 'Ere we go again – big words, meant to make us feel small.

**LYSETTE** Only if you let them. Subversive means it could turn the world upside down, right, Miss Bolton?

**MISS BOLTON** Something like that, Lysette.

**Mrs Burke** Exactly. It's bleedin' revolution, that's what it is. So if you takes my 'ubby's advice, 'eadmaster, you'll ban the book and slam the author up in jail for the next two 'undred years.

*The spotlight follows* **Mr. Jackson** *as he resumes his centre-stage position.*

**Jackson** That, of course, is exactly what the English government attempted to do, Tom, on the publication of your book. But you were warned in time – by your friend, the poet William Blake, who cannot be with us this evening as he is doing a school reading in *(the name of the school reading/performing this play)*. Thus forewarned, you took the boat for France.

**Celine** Mr. Lester, why haven't we got a constitution in this country?

**Lester** Because, my dear, you would not understand if it got up and bit you. And who put such an idea into your head?

**Sonja** My Gran's worried sick over her constitution.

**Paine** A nation without a constitution is a nation without liberty.

**Julian** Well there I have an answer for you, children. That is what distinguishes us British, the fact that we have rights without a constitution.

**Mrs Burke** A noble concept. That goes to the 'eart of my dear 'ubby's theories. Those as knows best, knows best, an' they're the ones already in charge.

**Lester** Exactly! Some of us have worked hard to get where we are. If 11C would only do their homework, who knows how their careers might advance?

*Suddenly there is the blast of an organ, preferably with orchestral accompaniment, playing the American national anthem, The Stars and Stripes.*

**Angel** Heaven calling! Gabriel to Ground Control…

*The studio lights dim and the spotlight picks out an* ***Angel*** *at stage rear, standing high up on one of the step-ladders.*

**Lester** More damned electronics!

**Angel** General George Washington with a message of greeting to Mr. Thomas Paine, author, father of the American Constitution –

**Washington** *on the other side of the steps.* ***Washington*** *is wearing a Stetson. He has, for preference, a deep Southern drawl.* Hey, hang on, Gabe – don't overdo it. *(doffs his Stetson)* How-di, Tom?

**Paine** Mister President – how's Heaven?

**Washington** There you go again, son – sour grapes. But no more of that, eh, Babe? After all, This *Was* Your Life.

**Jackson** General George Washington, ladies and gentlemen – first president of the United States.

*Cheers and clapping from the audience.* ***Washington*** *swaggers forward into the centre circle of the studio. To go with, and compete with, his Stetson, he might wear the uniform of the cavalry, but with spurs that clink noisily. Hanging from his belt, but trailing on the ground, is a cavalry sword.*

And your message, Mister President?

**Washington** Yeah, Tom did his bit. When we Yankees were up against it during the War of Independence – icy winds across the Delaware, when the Brits outnumbered us and we looked into the mouth of slaughter. *(slaps his thigh)* As sure as my body lies in Mount Vernon, and my spirit with the Good Shepherd, but for Tom there and his writing – his inspiration, we'd still be singing Rule Britannia.

102 **Jackson** You never actually gave Tom the vote, though, did you?

**Washington** We gave him a house to live in. That was something, considering the cost of real estate these days.

**Jackson** But on his death, in poverty, neglected, you did not even send a representative to his funeral.

**Washington** Affairs of state, my friend. And there was his other book. Not so popular with us good people who pray every day and reap the Lord's harvest.

**Paine** I attacked the church, not the practice of prayer.

**Jackson** We are referring here to Tom's last great masterpiece, 'The Age of Reason' –

**Washington** Not very friendly to people in authority, I am afraid.

**Jackson** So for all his contribution to the success of the American revolution, for inventing the very term, The United States of America, he was thrust out into the cold.

**Washington** Believe me, Tom, Babe, Heaven wouldn't suit you. Twenty-four hours up here and you'd have even the angels striking for more pay. They're a pain in the ass as it is.

**Miss Bolton** There was the little matter of slavery, Mr. President.

**Washington** *looks her up and down* Mmm – short skirts would never 'a' bin tolerated in my day. *(shakes his head)* Yeah, Tom got a bit of a bore about it, but we had our priorities, Missy – the economy. The abolition of slavery, well, that and better roads and improved parking facilities, it just had to wait.

**Paine** To your everlasting shame, Mr. President.

**Washington** See what I mean? – a goddam Red Commy terrorist to the end!

*As **Washington** returns to his place on the steps, The Stars and Stripes sounds once more.*

**Jackson** Applause, ladies and gentlemen, for America's very first president.

*Applause.*

**Washington** *to the **Angel*** Hey, Gabe, how come they don't have short skirts in heaven?

*The light fades on him.*

**Voice 1** Bloody Yanks, think they own the place.

**Washington** *from a far distance* I heard that!

**Jackson** *turning his attention back to* ***Tom Paine*** In England, Sir, you were tried in your absence and found guilty of treason, likely to be hanged, drawn and quartered if captured, your head stuck on a spike on Tower Hill.

*Sound of a mobile phone.*

**Julian** Sorry, everyone – cabinet business.

**Jackson** We're on TV, Sir Julian, for heaven's sake.

**Julian** *speaking into the phone* Yes, Prime Minister. No, Prime Minister. Absolutely, Prime Minister. *(pauses. Approaches the audience as viewers)* Ladies and gentlemen, I very much regret that this programme is to be pulled out of the schedules.

**Sonja** That sounds painful, Jules.

**Julian** On the orders of the Home Office.

**Miss Bolton** I've had a bad feeling about this all evening. They're switching us off, Jeth.

**Julian** This programme is breaking the law, by giving air time to a convicted criminal –

**Jackson** That's nonsense!

**Julian** Mr. Thomas Paine was found guilty of seditious libel. *(shouts)* Seditious libel! – and outlawed from setting foot on English soil ever again.

**Jackson** *furious* That was in 1792!

**Julian** The law must take its course: the sentence still stands. This is an illegal assembly. Officers?

***Voice 1*** *and* ***Voice 2*** *stand up. They are secret agents. We might now see them in dark macks. They place trilbies on their heads.*

**Voice 1** Yes, Sir, three bags full, Sir.

**Voice 2** *produces a weapon, a short automatic familiar in police series. Waves it round the room* Nobody leave this studio.

**JULIAN** *pointing at* ***Tom Paine*** Arrest that man.

**VOICE 1** It'll be our pleasure, Minister.

**LYSETTE** Russell – help us get Tom away. Tom!

**TONY** I feel a riot coming on.

**MITCHELL** Me too.

**IMRAN** Come on, 11C!

*Lights flash on and off as a scrimmage ensues – a veritable battle as Authority seeks to apprehend* ***Tom Paine*** *and* ***Form 11C*** *strives to ensure his escape.*

**DENISE** Bless you Tom!

**CELINE** From now on, you're my Uncle Tom.

**SONJA** Mine too!

*Suddenly there is a single, deafening pistol shot. The combatants freeze.*

**VOICE 2** *shouting* Down on yer faces – everybody – on yer faces!

***Everyone*** *hits ground and as they do so, all the lights go out. For a moment there is silence.*

**CELINE** This is scary.

**VOICE 1** Silence!

**SIR JULIAN** Nobody will get hurt. So long as the prisoner is handed over.

*Silence.*

**LYSETTE** *in the dark* Take my hand, Tom.

**VOICE 1** Halt, or I fire! Ouch!

**RUSSELL** What did I say 'bout that knuckle sarny?

**Voice 1** Je-sus, that hurt!

**Voice 2** I got 'im, Boss!

**Lester** That's my leg – unhand me this instant! Allow me to deal with this matter, Julian. *(pause)* Julian?

**Miss Bolton** That's me. Mr. Lester. Take your hand off my bosom at once.

**Sonja** This is a whole lot better than FOFO, Mr. Jackson.

**Lester** FOFO?

**Tony** F-off and find out, Sir. That's education.

***Mr Jackson** is now at the front of the stage. In a single spotlight, he stares out at the audience.*

**Jackson** In London, Tom, a paid mob burns your effigy. They carry aloft a banner on which is written, 'Behold a Traitor!' You take ship for France where, at Calais, you are greeted by brass bands.

*We hear another national anthem, this time that of France, 'The Marseillaise'.*

Such is your fame that you are appointed to the House of Deputies, smothered with honours. Yet you soon run into trouble with those who once favoured you, because you oppose the death sentence upon the King, Louis XVI.

*A second spotlight picks out **Tom Paine**, to the rear of the stage, his arms hooked into those of **Lysette** and **Russell**. They are framed against the arch among the ruins on the school playing field.*

***Mr. Jackson** moves to stage right.*

**Paine** Yes, as I opposed the death sentence at all times.

**Jackson** Suddenly you are no longer welcome among the revolutionaries. You are arrested. You are taken to the Luxemburg prison. You are sentenced to death. The dreaded guillotine awaits you.

**Mrs Burke** *at stage left* Ooh, I do love an execution!

*The stage lights return, creating a strobe-like effect. They reveal a hang-headed* ***Form 11C*** *in weary procession. One of the step-ladders is now front of stage; these are the stairs leading up to the guillotine. The procession halts. All eyes now turn to look upwards.*

**Lester** *appearing in the place of* ***Mrs. Burke****, stage left* I think this may solve our little problem, Jesse. After all, 11C had it coming to them.

*We hear the fearsome sound of the guillotine.* ***Form 11C*** *yell in shock and dismay. The lights go out once more.*

**Tony** *in the dark* That was no Stanley knife!

## Scene Seven

*The Luxemburg prison, Paris. There is the opportunity here for a little stage 'mist'. If there is to be scenery, then we are in a cell with an open door leading on to a corridor. Boxes can easily be used to simulate this set.*

*Darkness. The sound of the guillotine is now very close and as regular as the striking of a clock.*

**Lysette** *scared* Russell?

**Russell** That's me – where are we?

**Paine** Don't be afraid.

**Lysette** Tom? Oh heavens, where are we?

**Paine** Paris, the prison of the Luxemburg.

**Russell** We're dreaming.

**Paine** I hope so. But for me this is the last stage of my journey. I shall shortly be taken to the guillotine. This *Was* Your Life, Tom Paine.

*Sound of the guillotine.*

**LYSETTE** It's getting closer. This is no dream.

**RUSSELL** It'll be the end of 'is dreams when I get my 'ands on Julian 'icks.

**PAINE** Over a hundred prisoners, many of them my friends, have been executed this week.

**RUSSELL** What's goin' to 'appen to us, Tom?

**PAINE** Even the world's cleverest tyrants cannot kill those who have not yet been born.

**LYSETTE** Then how did we get here?

**PAINE** On wings of imagination, my dear. And empathy.

**RUSSELL** More long words – what's that mean?

**PAINE** A fellow feeling. You have stepped into my shoes, into my existence. I'm sorry.

*From the distance, down the corridor of the prison, comes the sound of the slamming of iron doors.*

**PAINE** It looks as though they are coming for me.

**RUSSELL** Tom, you were the 'ero, they played brass bands for you. 'Ow's it all changed so fast?

**PAINE** Alas, revolutions often fall into the hands of fanatics. Yet until now Monsieur Robespierre has hesitated to execute a friend of the United States.

**LYSETTE** George Washington – can't he help?

**PAINE** I have written to him. He has not yet replied.

*A corner of the stage is spotlighted.* ***President Washington*** *is at* ***Mr. Lester****'s desk.* ***Mrs. Draper*** *approaches.*

**MRS DRAPER** Mr. President?

**WASHINGTON** Not now, Babe.

**Mrs Draper** I was just wondering whether you'd had time to think about that letter from –

**Washington** Not Tom Paine again? –

**Mrs Draper** Well, it looks like the Frogs are going to chop his head off unless you put in a word for him.

**Washington** And interfere in the politics of another country? There are times to speak out, and times to stay mum, Mrs. Draper. That's called diplomacy.

**Mrs Draper** *in a low voice* I'd call it ingratitude.

**Washington** What was that, Babe?

*The spotlight is extinguished. The sound of the slamming doors gets closer.*

**Paine** My young friends, do you remember how we strolled together under the stone arch at Fort Pox? Well … this building was once a grand palace. There is another arch.

**Lysette** We're not just going to walk out on you.

**Russell** Y'can come back with us, Tom – through the same arch. Just think what you could teach the world.

**Paine** On the contrary, you young people have been the teachers. I have learnt much from you. Tell me, please – it'll help calm my nerves – about what you, Lyse, called the Web. How poetic and inspiring that sounds – the World Wide Web; people of all classes and races talking to one another free of the curse of kings and popes … I see a new world.

**Lysette** Not if our headmaster has anything to do with it.

**Russell** There's this meetin'. 'E's goin' to kick us off the Web.

**Paine** Then you must return at once.

*Slamming of doors is now almost deafening.*

At once, my young friends. The rights of man –

**Lysette** And of women, Tom!

**Paine** Of course. The rights of man and woman are constantly under threat. There will always be those who would guillotine them, chop off the heads of Justice and Liberty.

**Russell** In a way that's what they're wantin' to do with us –

**Lysette** With my article. Though in this horrible cell, all that seems so, so – trivial.

**Paine** Courage, my child – great causes are won by small battles. And they are lost by seemingly trivial defeats.

**Lysette** Yet Julian Hicks says we must compromise or our magazine and our website will be shut down altogether.

**Paine** Compromise in such matters, Lysette, is surrender. *(he laughs)* And now you know, my friends, why I am not on your National Curriculum.

*Closest slamming of the door. A spotlight illuminates* ***Tom Paine****. He speaks out towards the audience.*

**Paine** Perhaps if I had compromised a little more I would be a rich and successful senator, taking tea and muffins with George Washington. I have no regrets – except ... (*he turns towards his young friends)* – to lose your friendship, members of 11C. Youth is the seedtime of good habits, as well in nations as in individuals. Go forth and battle for what is right. Now, away with you, through the arch.

**Russell** Talkin' of right – this isn't right. Us doin' a runner.

**Paine** Do it! The present time is the true time.

**Lysette** A hug, Tom. *(she hugs him)* Thank you, for everything.

***Jailer*** *enters.*

**Jailer** *bellowing* Next for the chop!

*Lights fade.*

## Scene Eight

*The Headmaster's study.* ***Mr. Lester*** *is sitting exactly where George Washington was seated in the last scene.* ***Mr. Jackson*** *and* ***Miss Bolton*** *stand nervously to attention.*

**LESTER** Now I wish to be absolutely clear which side you two are going to be on in this Meeting. Are you for us, or against us, with regard to the school magazine and website? 102

**JACKSON** I didn't realise that taking sides, Headmaster, was what all this is about.

**LESTER** Don't come the innocent with me, Jesse.

**JACKSON** Jethro, Sir.

**LESTER** Just remember you are still on trial – probation – for the next six months.

**MISS BOLTON** I hope that we can be relied on to show a sense of balance, Headmaster.

**LESTER** What's that supposed to mean? Might I remind you, Miss Bolton, that it is well known among the school governors that you have been writing the coursework on 'Romeo and Juliet' for Form 11C.

**MISS BOLTON** How else are they going to get their GCSEs in English, Mr. Lester? None of them does any work. And you told school – we climb the league tables or die.

*Enter* ***Mrs Draper****.*

**MRS DRAPER** Excuse me, Headmaster, but Lady Testard has just arrived.

**LESTER** Good. And Mr. Paine?

**MRS DRAPER** The Inspectorate have phoned in, Sir – a Mr. Robes-Pierre, sounded rather foreign. Mr. Paine is indisposed.

**LESTER** Wonderful! Who said prayers aren't answered? Indisposed, eh? *(mockingly)* Mr. Paine is indisposed. Too much contact with

11C, I guess. Well let's hope it isn't terminal. You know what this means, Jesse?

**JACKSON** That in the meeting you'll have a clear run?

**LESTER** A clear run – exactly. Now show these people out, Mrs. Draper, and make a nice cup of coffee for the Chairman of Governors and myself. You may use the brown sugar for our guest. It's not often I have good news for Lady Testard. *(he laughs)* Mr. Paine – is indisposed!

## Scene Nine

***Russell*** *and* ***Lysette*** *are escaping from the Luxemburg. In a production they race, in the semi-dark, along 'passages' of boxes. In a reading, they simulate breathlessness. A shrill drumbeat has taken the place of the swish of the guillotine.*

***Lysette*** *stops abruptly.*

**RUSSELL** Come on, Lys – what's up?

**LYSETTE** I'm sorry – I'm not going.

**RUSSELL** Not goin'?

*The drumbeat fades.*

**LYSETTE** I'm not deserting him. Tom Paine's become our friend.

**RUSSELL** But 'e said it 'imself – 'e's 'istory, we're Now. Anyway, all this 'as got to be an 'orrible nightmare.

**LYSETTE** Suit yourself. Don't you see, though, if Tom dies now – there'll be no more of his books.

**RUSSELL** Talkin' of books at this time? – you're crazy.

**LYSETTE** It helps. So you push off if you want to.

*Enter the* ***Jailer****, shaking heavy keys.*

**JAILER** Hey, you boy – Garçon!

*He rattles his keys loudly.*

**Lysette** Oh God – he's seen us.

**Russell** Run, then –

**Jailer** Garçon!

**Russell** Lyse – stay there. Freeze. 'E's not seen you, only me.

**Jailer** Venez ici, Garçon. Tout suite, at the double.

**Russell** *whispering* What's 'e sayin'?

**Lysette** He wants you to go to him.

**Jailer** 'Ere, Kid. Save me legs. Do some chalkin'.

**Russell** Chalkin'?

**Jailer** See the numbers on all them doors? That means they're for the chop-chop tomorrer. Number four for Old Tom Paine. Pity, cos for an Englishman, allowin' for the fact that the Brits 're generally a bunch o' tossers, he's bin a real decent bloke.

But Mon-sur Robespierre – nasty little git, only 'im bein' in charge for the moment we gotta do as 'e says. Citizen Bleedin' Robespierre can't stand Tommy's ideas about mur-cy. So 'ere's the chalk. Now write it big so there's no mistake or mi 'own 'ead'll be rollin' in't' basket.

**Russell** Number four?

**Jailer** That's the one, Kid. I'll finish off down 'ere.

**Lysette** *whispering* Don't do it. Russell? *(pause. The drumbeat returns.* ***Russell*** *darts away into shadow)* Russell?

**Jailer** *from a distance* Done it, Son? Nice and large?

**Russell** Nice and large, Mon-sure.

**Jailer** Number four?

**Russell** Number four. Big as a dinner plate.

**Lysette** I'll never forgive you.

**RUSSELL** One day, if we ever get out o' this – you'll understand. 'Onest, Lyse – trust me.

**LYSETTE** To what?

**RUSSELL** To 'ave done somethin' intelligent for once.

*From distant cells come screams of fear and weeping – these being provided by an invisible **Form 11C.***

**JAILER** *calling* Don't worry, Folks, Madame Guillotine'll dry yer tears.

## Scene 10

*In semi-darkness, **Lysette** and **Russell** race down the corridors of the Luxemburg; as footlights come on these are transformed into the corridors of William Pitt School. At front of stage they almost collide with **Mr Jackson**.*

**JACKSON** Where've you two been? The meeting's already started.

**RUSSELL** Y' wouldn't believe us if we told you, JackoSir.

**JACKSON** Well get in there.

**LYSETTE** I want to know something, Sir.

**JACKSON** It'll have to wait. Now, please.

**LYSETTE** What happened to Tom, Sir – I mean, when he was in prison in Paris?

**JACKSON** Lysette, forget our Project for the time being. This is a crisis, for you, for me, for the school.

**LYSETTE** But Mr. Jackson –

**JACKSON** I'll tell you later. Now inside, both of you.

*They enter the Consultative Meeting to be greeted with loud cheers and wolf whistles from **Form 11C**.*

*The set is once again made up of boxes, this time in a V-formation opening out towards the audience. On a row of two or three boxes at the point of the V is a desk, behind which sits* ***Mr. Lester****,* ***Lady Testard*** *and* ***Mrs. Draper****, taking the Minutes.*

*On the desk is a jug of water and a glass.*

***Form 11C*** *are seated on chairs along the arms of the V, the boys (****Tony****,* ***Imran*** *and* ***Mitchell****) on one side, the girls (****Denise****,* ***Celine*** *and* ***Sonja****) on the other.*

*At the end of the girls' row, with a couple of spare chairs between her and the students, is* ***Miss Bolton****. Opposite her, with a couple of spare chairs between him and the boys, sits* ***Julian Hicks****, smartly dressed compared to his peers.*

**LESTER** *in response to the prolonged cheers* Quiet!

**CELINE** Love's young dream.

***Lysette*** *and* ***Russell*** *separate, he to sit with the girls, she with the boys.*

**TONY** Oh Romeo, Romeo – where fart thou?

**LESTER** I said – shut up.

***Miss Bolton*** *moves up a place for* ***Mr Jackson*** *to sit down.*

**JACKSON** You okay?

**MISS BOLTON** Ask me that when this meeting's over.

**DENISE** Nobody should say shut up to Shakespeare, Sir. Should they, Miss Bolton?

**LADY TESTARD** Very amusing – but shall we proceed?

**MITCHELL** You think Shakespeare was a queer, don't you, Miss Bolton?

**LESTER** That's enough, 'Moon.

**IMRAN** It doesn't matter. We're all human beings – aren't we, Mr. Jackson?

**Sonja** My Gran gets queer turns. Specially when she forgets to light the gas. The other day –

**Lester** Order, order! *(turns to the **Chairman of the Governors**)* Lady Testard. This young lady *(he points towards **Lysette**)* … Lysette Thomas, is editor of the 11C section of our school magazine. And Russell Morgan is, er –

**Tony** A criminal!

**Lysette** I'm also deputy editor of the whole magazine, Sir, and in charge of the website, which I designed with Imran.

**Imran** And we're really proud of it.

**Lysette** I'm sorry I'm late. We were seeing off our friend to the scaffold.

**Lady Testard** Scaffold?

**Lysette** We arrive back and what's the score? The guillotine is hanging over our magazine.

**Imran** And our website. After all, Lyse, that's the most important, 'cos we can talk to the world – without interference.

**Lester** That is what we are here to decide, Hardy.

**Tony** I'm Hardy, Sir, that's Jayasingh. Only I'm called Hard*ing*. So no kiss-me-quick jokes if you don't mind.

**Mitchell** Here, that's my line. In fact, what I'd like to know is why there isn't more homosexuality in schools.

**Lester** *testily* Because your betters have seen fit to ban it by Act of Parliament.

**Lysette** Can we keep to the point of this meeting, Headmaster?

**Lester** Thank you, Lysette. That is my intention.

**Russell** The point is simple. *(he stands)* We don't want no tamperin' wi' our magazine. 'StirCrap's' not got to be censored, not in any way. Not one word. Not one picture, just because of a ruddy inspection. No compromise!

*Cheers of support from* ***11C. Russell*** *acknowledges the applause and sits down.*

**Lester** We were in fact on item two of the agenda: leaky taps in the senior girls' lavatories.

**Lady Testard** 'StirCrap'? I thought the magazine was called 'Forward'.

**Lester** Taps, Mi-Lady.

**Tony** Crap not taps.

**Jackson** Shut it, Tony.

**Lester** Might we at least settle the matter of leaky taps?

**Mrs Draper** There's a plumber coming tomorrow, Sir.

**Lester** Excellent, Mrs. Draper. So these little problems will be sorted out prior to the Inspection.

**Mrs Draper** And he's going to fix the electrics while he's at it.

**Lester** Is he qualified to do both?

**Mrs Draper** He managed the sports pavilion roof all right.

**Tony** What's his name – Draper?

**Lester** Order! *(confused)* Now where were we?

**Lady Testard** Mud, Headmaster.

**Lester** Mud, Mi-Lady?

**Lady Testard** Item six on the agenda – mud.

**Lester** Mud – of course! Mud being trampled over the floors in reception, not to mention empty crisp bags littering every corner of the quadrangle.

**Lysette** Mr. Lester, we are here to discuss censorship. The banning of our magazine. Not taps, not mud or litter. Not rules and regulations. Otherwise I'm off for a fag.

**Lester** Lysette, the agenda of this meeting specifically specifies –

**Lysette** And who drew up the agenda, Sir? This is just a silly tactic to put things off, to delay talking about what we're really here for.

**Lady Testard** *impatiently* Let her carry on, Headmaster. It seems she will whether we permit her or not.

**Lester** Very well, Mi-Lady. We shall proceed to item thirteen on the agenda.

**Denise** Thirteen is actually my lucky number.

**Sonja** My sister was pregnant thirteen times before she had her first baby.

**Lester** Order, order!

**Sonja** Oh, I don't know what order they were in, though she later had twins twice on the trot.

**Celine** I don't like that word – order. It means 'you got to' and if a boy says that to me I drop him like a hot brick.

**Tony** But if he says 'Please', you drop your pants quicker than –

**Jackson** Tony – belt up!

**Celine** *on her feet, crossing the floor* He's not going to get away with that.

*She lays in to* ***Tony*** *who has to be protected by* ***Imran*** *and* ***Mitchell****. They duck under her blows, only for* ***Miss Bolton*** *to settle the fight by pulling* ***Celine*** *free.*

**Miss Bolton** Cool it, Celine! *(she draws* ***Celine*** *gently back to the girls' side)* How many times have I told you, ignore a prick and he deflates faster than a spent balloon.

**Lester** Miss Bolton – I didn't hear that remark

**Celine** *resuming her seat* Thanks, Miss, for reminding me. *(she suddenly jabs her arm out in the direction of* ***Tony****)* If I was you I'd spend my drugs money on a bodyguard in future.

**Tony** *contrite, possibly a little scared* Sorry Celine.

**Lysette** *angry with her peers* Are we going to get serious for once or aren't we?

**Julian** Time is moving on, Headmaster.

**Lester** Thank you, Julian. *(clears his throat. Waits. There is silence)* That's better. Now … I think on the matter of a magazine title, Julian, as the editor, ought to have his say. (turns to ***Lady Testard***) Julian Hicks, Mi-lady. Our head prefect.

**Lady Testard** We are acquainted. How is your father, Julian?

**Celine** Ooh! *(aping **Lady Testard**)* How's your father?

**Tony** *chanting* All right!
Saw 'im in the fish queue – last night!

***Celine** and **Tony** exchange smiles. Their feud is over.*

**Julian** Keeping well, My Lady, though I hardly ever see him.

**Denise** Except on telly.

**Julian** *rather sadly* That's true, Denise.

**Denise** Call me Den.

**Julian** Thanks.

**Lester** Now, Julian.

**Mitchell** How come, Sir, it's Julian for him an' last names for the rest of us?

**Miss Bolton** Please, Mitch, allow the meeting to go ahead.

**Mitchell** For you, Miss Bolton – anything!

**Lester** Julian – your views, please.

**Julian** Well, Sir, on careful consideration –

**Celine** We know what's going to happen to you, Julian, in the future.

**Jackson** Celine!

**Celine** It's true, Sir. He's going to be a big shot in the government.

**Russell** Yeah, a real arsehole.

**Lysette** Russell!

**Russell** Sorry.

**Julian** What we want, as students writing and editing a magazine, is important. But it's not the only thing we should think about. There's the readership – the people out there. Students, yes, but also parents.

**Sonja** Got no parents!

**Jackson** *warningly* Sonja – listen.

**Julian** We have to consider how we're coming over, what people think of us.

**Russell** They think we're rubbish, so the magazine couldn't 'ave a better title.

**Lysette** Aren't we all getting hung up about a title? What counts is what's *in* the magazine. What its views are. Whether it's just a load of smarmy butter – or whether it's about important things, things that matter in our lives, things that reach out – yeah – reach out for the truth.

**Lester** *in a superior tone* Ah, the truth, a many-splendoured thing, Lysette. Alas, who can define it?

**Lysette** We can try, Sir.

**Lester** Julian – we cut you off.

**Lysette** *swiftly, assertively* Don't say it, any of you. Go on, Julian, you've started so you'd better finish.

**Julian** Thanks, Lysette. *(pause)* Why are we here – at the school, I mean?

**Celine** Because we have to be, stupid.

**Julian** I asked – Why?

*Silence.*

**Sonja** So we're not out of our 'eads on crack all day, dancin' on the ceilin'?

*Laughter.*

**Julian** *triumphantly* The reason is – so that we can turn out how we want to be. But responsibly.

**Lester** Bravo, young man.

**Russell** *standing abruptly* Bollocks!

**Lester** Sit down, Morgan.

**Lysette** Yes, sit down.

***Russell** thinks about it, then sits.*

**Lester** Now where were we, Julian?

**Lysette** Okay, Sir, we know where Jules is coming from. It's Russell's turn.

**Form 11C** *together* Yeah!

**Mitchell** Sock it to 'em, Russ.

**Lester** *shrugs* Keep it clean, Morgan, and keep it brief.

**Lysette** Go on, Russ.

**Russell** Well, accordin' to slippery Jules 'ere.

**Julian** *darting to his feet* I object to that comment.

**Celine** Oh shut up, Jules. Russ's being kind – most of us call you Slippery Dick.

**Julian** *sitting down but still angry. He appeals to the Headmaster* Sir!

**Lady Testard** Order!

**Russell** Yeah, Misses – that's my point: order. Orders is all we ever get. *(he slowly returns to his feet)* What's it all mean, eh? It's okay for Jules. 'E knows where 'e's goin'. But the rest of us, we're 'ere to be turned out like other people want us to be. An'above all –

kept in order. Like Lyse says in her article. *(he stares around him, glances at **Lysette** who nods approvingly. He sits down)* Like – spend up or shut up. 'Cos that's all that counts these days, an' if we're skint, as most of us are, we count for nothin'.

**Celine** Good on you, Russ – you're not such a ball-brain after all.

**Jackson** Maybe you're right, Russell. The consumerist society enchains us all. But you could argue that education liberates you.

**Mitchell** I don't feel liberated. Fact is, this dump is a factory churning out folks to be identical –

**Jackson** Because you resist it – resist what it can do for you.

**Tony** Hey, Sir – we're 11C. The no-hopers.

**Miss Bolton** I was in a sink class all my days at school, so I understand what Russell is getting at.

**Lester** Thank you, Miss Bolton, but we do have a pressing agenda.

**Russell** There you go – Miss Bolton's got a degree, but she's not liberated. None of you are. I mean, look at you, teachers 'avin' nervous breakdowns all over the shop 'cos there's a stupid inspection round the corner.

**Julian** Headmaster, isn't all this about, er – standards?

**Lester** *as if he needed reminding* Of course, of course, Julian – standards!

**Julian** Without inspections, Headmaster, things like what Lysette reveals in her article might continue.

**Lysette** *assertively* Which brings us to the main point. Things wrong have to be put right. Right, Julian?

**Julian** *uncertain, uneasy about publicly agreeing with anything **Lysette** says and fearing a trap* Er, right.

**Lysette** *triumphantly* But not if the contents of my article are kept secret, Jules. Censorship hides what's wrong. It is the enemy of standards – right?

**JULIAN** *realising that he has made a rather dangerous point* Yes, I s'pose...

**LESTER** *sharply* Whose side are you on, Hicks?

**LYSETTE** Thanks, Julian, for making our case for freedom.

**JULIAN** *uncertain* Have I?

**LYSETTE** You have. Because if Mr Lester has his way, when the inspectors arrive at school the truth about it will be hidden. Stuffed under the carpet.

**TONY** Under the floorboards more like.

**LESTER** Oh no they won't!

**FORM 11C** *in chorus, standing, waving their arms* Oh yes they will!

**LESTER** *shouting* Sit down, all of you at once!

*They all sit down.*

**JULIAN** Sir, I wasn't actually suggesting we sweep things under the carpet.

**FORM 11C** *in unison* Oh yes you were!

**LYSETTE** *quietly* What else could you have been suggesting, Julian? You want us to hold things over; and if we do, and when everything goes quiet – there'll still be those who want to shut our mouths.

*She stands, steps down from the box. She walks to the end of the row so that she can address the whole meeting, while at the same time glancing now and then out towards the audience.*

Come the inspection, sure we'll all behave – because we like Mr. Jackson and Miss Bolton. We'll ask intelligent questions. We'll not gob out of the window, swear, put our feet up on the desk. We'll quote Shakespeare. We'll all say how much we enjoyed studying the Dead Sea Scrolls and Domesday Book, and Miss Bolton's lessons on contraception when she ought to be training us up to pass our English Language. *(glancing at* ***Miss Bolton****)* Thanks, Lorna, we appreciate it. *(pause)* Don't worry, we'll say the right things. We'll behave. The boys'll shove their hands up in the air instead of up the girls' pants and we'll all come out smelling of roses, get a good report – but the rotten things will go on as usual.

**Mrs. Draper** Am I supposed to get all this down, Headmaster?

**Lester** Of course not, merely the main points.

**Lysette** *angry now; waves arms despairingly* But I'm *making* the main points!

**Lady Testard** I am anxious, Headmaster, to bring this matter to a close.

**Lester** Of course, of course, Mi-Lady. Your other pressing engagements. Thank you, Lysette. You may sit down now.

***Lysette** hesitates, then shakes her head. She sits, but on the edge of her chair.*

**Lady Testard** I wish to remind those present that decisions which affect the school are the responsibility of the governors – alone – in consultation with the head.

**Tony** Then this meeting's just a sham?

**Lester** We have heard your views –

**Form 11C** *With the exception of **Lysette, Form 11C** stand, demonstrate a Mexican wave* Oh no you haven't!

**Lester** *bellowing* Sit down. I won't have anarchy in my school.

**Imran** Anarchy, Sir? I'm not with you.

**Lester** What we've got here at this moment – chaos.

*There is a brief silence as if those present are uncertain what must happen next.*

**Lady Testard** *clearing her throat* Very well, I think we are agreed, then, that in the absence of Mr. Paine who I believe wished to address this meeting –

**Lester** But for his indisposition, yes indeed, Mi-Lady –

**Lady Testard** – that common sense, not to mention discretion, demands we take this opportunity to hold over the school magazine and the web site till the inspection is complete.

**Lysette** *leaps to her feet* That's not been agreed. On what grounds do you want to censor my work, *(with contemptuous emphasis)* Mi-Lady?

**Lady Testard** *keeping calm* On the grounds that it is inflammatory –

**Russell** Insanitary? It bloody isn't!

**Lady Testard** Inflammatory, sensational, biased – and abominably spelt.

**Lester** I couldn't have put it better myself, Mi-Lady.

**Lysette** But what it says is true!

**Lester** *trying conciliation* Oh, Lysette, if you only understood how complicated life for adults can be. You won't necessarily believe it but once upon a time I was a nice person. A good headmaster. I had radicalism in my blood. Then they brought in the league tables –

**Tony** And you've been a little Hitler ever since.

*There is a tense silence.*

**Lester** To be perfectly honest with you – yes.

**Lysette** Then support us, Mr. Lester, and be free.

**Form 11** *loudly, together* Yeah!

**Lester** *it is his turn to stand up* Truth, freedom – they're not so easily purchased as a Big Mac. Now listen to me – please! If we publish, if we reach for freedom, if we tell the truth – we'll be damned. Believe me! And if I may be permitted to quote from the great philosopher, Schopenhauer –

**Tony** Oh not him again, Sir!

**Lester** 'Truth cannot appear naked before the people'. *(another silence)* Mr Jackson, you seem to have some credit with your form. I would appreciate it if you would put our case to them. *(he sits)*

102 **JACKSON** *getting up slowly. Sighs* I think … the Headmaster is saying, er, scandal, even if it is true, has sometimes … to be concealed … for the common good.

*Cries of disapproval from* ***11C****.*

Let me finish. Your article, Lysette, and the other bits and pieces that a few staff and governors object to, may be the truth. An uncomfortable truth. Things are wrong. They need to be put right. Isn't that correct, Headmaster?

**LESTER** Naturally.

**RUSSELL** Naturally my foot.

**JACKSON** *forcefully* Hear me out, Russ. *(he pauses)* Out there – out there, in the big wide world –

**LESTER** – the real world.

**TONY** It's a jungle, Sir – tell us something new.

**LYSETTE** Knowledge is power, Sir – didn't you teach us that?

**JACKSON** Yes, but it is a two-edged sword. It can be turned to use against us. *(he puts up his hands to quell murmurs of protest from* ***11C****)* Let's say the tabloid press gets hold of Lysette's story.

**LESTER** As well they might.

**JACKSON** What will they – the tabloids – do with it?

**LESTER** Crucify us!

**JACKSON** *firmly* I'm asking Form 11C, Headmaster.

**CELINE** Why don't they have completely naked men on Page 3, I'd like to know.

**MRS DRAPER** There was that case in Edmonton, Headmaster. They brought in private enterprise to take over the school.

**LESTER** Yes, thank you, Mrs. Draper, for reminding me of our possible fate.

**LYSETTE** *stands* No, I don't buy that, Mr. Jackson. No. *(she shakes her* *head)* Don't you see? One bit of censorship leads to another. If people get away with one bit, they'll try it on more next time. Then they'll start doing nasty things to people, because nobody speaks out. That makes things worse. A little bit of torture – why not? Nobody's going to say anything. Good grief, your next door neighbour's just disappeared. They came for him at four o'clock in the morning. Best not say anything or they'll come for you.

Heavens, Mr. Jackson – don't you remember that poem you read out to us?

**Denise** It was you too, Miss Bolton, who read us that poem.

**Imran** Yeah, how they came and arrested people one by one –

**Russell** An' the poet stood by an' did bugger all.

**Mitchell** Till they came for him!

**Miss Bolton** But no one's coming to arrest you in the middle of the night, any of you.

**Lysette** They're going to lock up our words, though, aren't they, Miss Bolton? *(nodding towards* ***Miss Bolton*** *and* ***Mr. Jackson****)* Both of you – get smart!

**Form 11C** *cheers*

**Tony** *stands, shoots up his arm* Lys for President!

**Russell** *stands, throws up both arms, with clenched fists* No censorship! Balls to the Ban!

**Form 11C** *in chorus, all standing* Balls to the ban!

**Lady Testard** *loudly, assertively, imperiously* Headmaster – enough! To be frank, I'm rather impressed by your Form 11C. They are not the dunderheads you said they were. As for Miss Thomas, well … She speaks intelligently and she has pluck. *(with great emphasis)* However, this debate will not affect the decision that the governors will take after due consideration. *(she stands)*

**Lester** *with relief* Of course – your pressing engagement, Mi-Lady. *(he stands)* We do still have the matter of the Carol Concert to sort out, but I think we'll be able to –

**RUSSELL** *loudly, threateningly* Sit down – Mi-lady! You too, 'Ector.

**JACKSON** *warningly* Russell!

**LADY TESTARD** Nobody speaks to me like that.

**RUSSELL** Well they do now, Misses. Sit!

*She does as she is told.*

**LESTER** This meeting is at an end.

**RUSSELL** *steps down from his chair and his box. Approaches the Head's table* Bum on the chair, 'Ector. This meetin's only just begun.

***Lester** sits in a state of shock. There is silence in the room.*

**JACKSON** Time to back off, I think, Russ. Tell him, Lyse.

**LYSETTE** *shakes her head* As Tom Paine said, the present time is the true time.

*She stands, pauses at the edge of her box.*

**RUSSELL** Time for *you* to back off, JackoSir. Fact is – nobody leaves till this matter's sorted. Mitch, Tony – the door.

***Tony** and **Mitchell** step from their boxes, hesitate.*

Go on – the door! It's now or never.

**TONY** Why not? It beats being preached at. Come on, Mitch.

**MITCHELL** If you say so, darlin'.

*They go to the door and stand guard.*

**LESTER** Morgan, what on earth are you doing?

**RUSSELL** Takin' 'ostages, that's what we're doin', 'eadmaster. Nobody legs it till we get what we want. An' that applies to you too, Mrs. Draper. No sneakin' out an' phonin' the pigs.

**Lady Testard** This is outrageous!

**Celine** I never realised meetings could be so exciting.

**Russell** Lys – what would Tom Paine think about this?

**Lester** I can imagine exactly how Inspector Paine will react to this situation. It is revolution!

**Lysette** I think he'd say – you get nothing in this world without fighting for it. That's what he told the Americans, didn't he, Mr. Jackson? When the Brits were beating them, and things looked black.

**Jackson** *uncertain how to respond* I ... well –

**Lysette** Wasn't that Tom Paine's way? Your hero. The greatest Englishman – ever? He believed in what was right, and nobody, not even George Washington – or God himself –

**Lady Testard** I wish to be released from this room – immediately. Or I shall summon the police. There will be serious charges, I assure you.

**Russell** Easy, Misses. I'm already up for grievous bodily 'arm next week, so don't give me no grief.

**Miss Bolton** I think I'm feeling ill.

**Sonja** It could be morning sickness, Miss. Me, I often get it in the afternoons.

**Julian** *half stands* I've just got to go to the loo – I'm bursting.

**Celine** Tie a knot in it.

**Julian** Please!

**Miss Bolton** A glass of water.

**Tony** It's certainly hot in here.

**Julian** You talk of freedom, but you won't even let me –

**Lester** Well said, Julian. Freedom of speech applies to all, not just to those who agree with you in the first place.

**Lysette** Okay, Russell, let him. We're not tyrants. Mitch, go with him. Don't let him out of your sight.

**Mitchell** But can I be trusted? Loos have a very peculiar effect on me.

**Denise** I think *I* want to go.

**Sonja** Me too. Weak bladders run in our family.

**Lysette** One at a time. Take him, Mitch. And bring him straight back.

***Mitchell** grabs **Julian's** arm, marches him off stage.*

**Mrs Draper** I don't know how I'm to get my work done, Headmaster, if I'm to remain cooped up –

**Lester** We're prisoners, Mrs. Draper. Letters can wait. Held hostage in my own school. A captive of Form 11C of all people.

**Russell** We're the dregs, Mr. Lester, what else d' y' expect?

**Lester** I expected more sense from you, Lysette.

**Lysette** Grant us our rights, Sir, and you'll be set free.

**Lester** Your rights?

**Lysette** To publish, to communicate, express ourselves, seek after the truth and tell it as it is. And perhaps most of all, grant us some respect!

***Julian Hicks** is hurled back on to stage by an angry **Mitchell**.*

**Mitchell** You bastard! He had a mobile phone, Lys. I think he's called the cops.

**Lester** Bravo, Julian!

*From the distance, a police siren; it is joined by a second, then a third. **Tony** joins **Mitchell** in manhandling **Julian**.*

**Julian** Stop it – stop it! – I didn't phone the police.

**TONY** Well that's no cock robin we're hearing.

**JULIAN** I didn't, I didn't phone the police. *(pause)* I phoned the press.

**LESTER** *in panic* You what, Hicks – the press?

**JULIAN** TV actually. My sister works with –

**LESTER** We don't want to hear about your sister, Hicks. This is perfidy.

**SONJA** Who says he's not lyin'?

**LESTER** Thank God the police will be here first. We'll simply deny everything to the press.

**LADY TESTARD** *desperately* I demand to be released at once. As a magistrate and chairman of the Police Committee I –

**RUSSELL** No passes out, I'm afraid. Only for the sick an' dyin'.

**LADY TESTARD** *she is on her feet. She swings her handbag defiantly* Out of my way. This handbag has scattered a dozen muggers in its time.

**JACKSON** Russ – do as she says. The police are probably already in the school drive. Don't make matters worse.

**MISS BOLTON** I think I'm going to faint.

***Denise** takes the water jug from the Headmaster's table.*

**DENISE** Here, Miss – you're dehigrated. Have a drink.

***Miss Bolton** accepts a glass of water gratefully.*

**JACKSON** Look, everybody – we can still rescue this situation. Let's agree – all this has been a – er – role play. 102

**LESTER** Role play? Have you taken leave of your senses, Jesse?

**JACKSON** A simulation, Sir, of the real thing: practice in how to handle problems. Part of our project on Tom Paine, even. How about it, class?

***Celine** has walked to the side of the stage, looks off stage as if glancing out of a window.*

**CELINE** That looks like the media all right. It's got Gay News TV written on the side.

**MITCHELL** Gay news? Fame at last. How'm I looking, Sonja?

**LESTER** You, Hicks, are suspended, as from this instant.

**LADY TESTARD** I'm waiting, Headmaster.

**JACKSON** How about it – a role play, a simulation – practice in democracy? – all a mistake –

**LESTER** You're a mistake, Jackson. *My* mistake was in taking you on in the first place. I should have trusted my gut instinct.

**CELINE** I reckon that's racism – you can't say things like that to JackoSir.

**LYSETTE** Forget it, Mr. Jackson, this is no role play. It's the real thing. Sorry about that. We can't pretend. My article says it all, and it's unravelling like a stinking ball of wool –

**IMRAN** Soaked in cat's pee –

**TONY** Like it!

**LYSETTE** We'll not be repressed – we'll not be suppressed –

**LESTER** But you will most certainly be locked up.

*The echo of boots along the school corridor. The sharp rap on the door takes on an echo as hints of the Luxemburg return. There is the sound of heavy keys opening heavy metal doors. The lights begin to flash.*

Whoever it is, Mrs. Draper, let them in.

**RUSSELL** I wouldn't advise it, Sir. If you want yer 'ead to stay on yer shoulders.

**TONY** You know what, killing is just what this play's been missing.

**MITCHELL** Come on – let's spill the ketchup and crunch a few bones. *(bellowing)* Action!

**LYSETTE** Steady on, Russ. We don't want to become like them.

**JULIAN** *with enthusiasm* Lyse – a business proposition. Forget 'Stircrap'. Tomorrow we'll be in every headline in the country. We'll be on TV. Fame! Before you know it, we'll all have agents. Our careers start right here.

**LYSETTE** Julian, you make me sick.

*A last crash of the prison door as the **Jailer** enters.*

**JAILER** *holding a list and staring about him* Chop-chop. Madame Guillotine wants 'er breakfast, or should I say petit de-jeun-er?

**LADY TESTARD** There you are at last, Jailer.

**JAILER** The next batch, is it, Citizen?

**LADY TESTARD** Citizen my foot. I am Lady Testard, second cousin of the Duchess of *(name of the local town or district) (she waves a dismissive hand at Form 11C)* Take them away. Form 11C – the lot of them. No mercy … no exceptions.

**LESTER** Detention would be sufficient, Mi-Lady.

**JAILER** Right, dummies. *(signals that they form a line. Reluctantly, nervously the **Students** make a line. They whisper)* No talkin' while I does me inspectin'! *(the **Jailer** pauses, glances again at his list, looks up)* 'Ang about, tho'… It don't say nothin' on me list 'bout juveniles. *(gazes at **Lady Testard**)* Fact is, this mornin' – it's bloated, fat-arsed aristocrats on mi list. Folks as sound their h's proper like. An' spell right, an' know where to put their apostroppy 's'. *(he points)* An' that's gotta be you, Ma-dame.

**FORM 11C** *cheers*

**DENISE** Honest, Mr. Jackson, this is definitely the best project ever!

*There is another knocking at the door. Enter **Reporter** with a camera slung around his or her neck.*

**REPORTER** *loudly* Evenin' all! I'm from the *(name of a local paper)*. I believe this school is revolting.

**Lester** *protesting* No it isn't!

**Form 11** *Call together* Oh yes it is!

*Lights out.*

## Scene 11

*Darkness except for a spotlight on* ***Lysette*** *and* ***Russell****. They appear to be in a police cell. As* ***Russell*** *speaks,* ***Mr. Jackson*** *enters the circle of light.*

**Russell** What're they goin' to charge us wi', JackoSir?

**Jackson** *shrugs* Hostage-taking, maybe. Kidnap. Hopeless idealism. Who knows?

**Lysette** At least we'll be out of harm's way – for the Inspection, that is.

**Russell** Not to mention yer project on Tom Paine, JackoSir, though it'll not be the same without us.

**Jackson** *sadly, resignedly* That's been dropped.

**Lysette** Banned, like Tom was?

**Jackson** Too political. Orders of the Headmaster. No Tom Paine at William Pitt School, I'm afraid; at least until the Inspection's over. And me, I'm on a first warning. Same as Miss Bolton.

**Lysette** We're sorry.

**Jackson** *shrugs* I was beginning to think we were getting somewhere.

**Russell** Just for the record, Jeth – what did 'appen to old Tom Paine? Did 'e cop it?

*There is the heavy slam of a steel door.*

**Jackson** *he sits beside them* Still interested, despite everything that's happened?

**LYSETTE** *nods* We kind of feel – responsible.

**JACKSON** *amused* Responsible?

**LYSETTE** Guilty, even.

**RUSSELL** Like, we let 'im down.

**JACKSON** You spoke up for what you think is right. No, you didn't let Tom Paine down.

*There is a pause. They are talking about different things.*

**LYSETTE** It all happened so quickly – in the Luxemburg, I mean. He was on the list, wasn't he, Mr. Jackson?

**JACKSON** Oh yes. Sentenced to death. Yet ... *(he hesitates, checks his enthusiasm)* All this ... *(he looks around him)* And you really want to know?

**RUSSELL** Yeah, we do – so what 'appened?

**JACKSON** A miracle.

*There is a silence. The sound of the haunting wind returns and then fades.*

A miracle! Truly... *(**Mr. Jackson** is suddenly energised, enthusiastic. He speaks as much to the audience as to **Lysette** and **Russell**)* That's the only way to describe it. A stroke of amazing luck.

***Mr. Jackson** stands, moving behind **Lysette** and **Russell** and staring out at the audience.*

**LYSETTE** Then he – wasn't?

**JACKSON** Guillotined? – no. *(pauses, addresses the audience)* Tom was in his cell. *(looks around him)* Not unlike this one, I imagine. Those who were to be taken for execution had numbers written on their doors.

**RUSSELL** In chalk?

**JACKSON** I guess so.

**LYSETTE** *decisively* It was chalk!

**JACKSON** Yet in the morning, as the guards came round – there was no number on Tom's door. Nothing. All the others had numbers, but not Tom's door. The other prisoners went to their death, but not Tom or the friends who shared his cell.

As I say, a miracle.

***Lysette*** *and* ***Russell*** *turn to each other, lock hands.*

**RUSSELL** How come, JackoSir?

***Tom Paine*** *enters in a white spotlight; at the same moment the light on* ***Mr. Jackson*** *fades.* ***Tom*** *now sits between* ***Russell*** *and* ***Lysette****.*

**PAINE** *speaking out towards the audience, the spotlight concentrated on his face* Yes, a bit of a miracle as Jethro says. The evening before, our cell door, which opened outwards into the corridor, had been left open.

***Russell*** *stands, mimes his own action, indicating the door flat against the wall. He writes the figure 4, then demonstrates how, when the door is shut, the number on the door is visible only to those on the inside.*

**LYSETTE** So Russell, you –

**PAINE** Chalked my number on the inside of the door, and of course when it was shut … *(he smiles)* No number! *(stands, touches the forehead of* ***Lysette*** *and* ***Russell*** *in turn as if to bless them and bid them farewell)* I owe you.

**LYSETTE** No, Tom – it's us who owe you.

**RUSSELL** *glowing* The rights of man!

**LYSETTE** And woman!

**PAINE** Of course.

*He begins to fade into darkness as illumination returns to* ***Mr. Jackson****.*

**JACKSON** The great man was spared, to write his last great work – 'The Age of Reason' –

**Paine** *from far off now* Which made me the most unpopular man in Christendom.

**Lysette** *desperately* Tom? – don't leave us. *(she stands, turns to capture a last glimpse of **Tom Paine**)* I only want to know – are we doing the right thing?

**Jackson** *looking after him into the wings* Yes, Tom – you were spurned in your old age. Even some of your friends turned their backs on you.

**Miss Bolton** *also stepping into the circle of light* Poor Tom, the world has never forgiven you. I'm beginning to know how you must have felt. You can speak the truth too much for your own good.

***Miss Bolton** steps out of the spotlight which now begins to flicker.*

**Jackson** We lesser mortals, well – we compromise. Tom Paine paid the price.

**Lysette** Like we're going to do.

*The sound of the wind returns; the present begins to dissolve once more into the past.*

**Jackson** At his funeral –

**Lysette** We'll be there, won't we, Russ?

*The stage is flooded with a stark, bleached light.The stage boxes form an oblong, leaving a space in the centre the shape of a grave. **Lysette** and **Russell** step up on to the boxes and stand on the right hand side of the grave.*

**Jackson** *remaining at corner stage* There were fewer than a dozen mourners, yet among them was the widow of an old friend from his days in France. Tom had helped with money and kindness: Madame Bonneville.

*From the wings, left, appears **Madame Bonneville**. She carries a garland of flowers. She goes to the head of the grave, for a second glancing out at the audience, then staring down at the coffin of the Greatest Englishman – ever.*

**Lysette** It's so cold.

**Jackson** New Rochelle – June 1809.

**Russell** Snuggle up to me, Lys.

***Miss Bolton*** *enters from stage left, leading* ***Form 11C****. She carries sprays of flowers, handing one each to her students as they walk slowly towards the grave and gather round it. Then she moves towards* ***Mr Jackson****, giving him a spray and a swift kiss on the cheek.*

*She crosses to the graveside, handing a spray each to* ***Lysette*** *and* ***Russell****. He at first refuses them (flowers he deems to be unmanly) but is gently but firmly obliged to receive them by* ***Lysette****.*

*Hesitant in the wings at stage right is* ***Julian****. He hangs his head but* ***Denise*** *steps down, takes his hand, and he joins the others at the graveside.*

***Madame De Bonneville*** *drops her flowers one by one into the grave.* ***Form 11C*** *do the same. As* ***Julian*** *has no flowers* ***Denise*** *gives him some of hers.*

*For a moment it appears that* ***Russell*** *is going to protest at* ***Julian****'s presence, but a warning tug on his arm from* ***Lysette*** *commands his silence and acceptance.*

*Meanwhile* ***Mr. Jackson*** *has crossed to join the mourners. He stands up stage from* ***Lysette*** *and* ***Russell****. As* ***Mr. Jackson*** *drops his spray of flowers in the grave, so does* ***Russell****.* ***Lysette*** *raises her flowers to her lips.*

***Madame De Bonneville*** *now looks up. Her gaze is fixed upon* ***Russell****.*

**Russell** Why's she starin' at me?

**Mme Bonneville** Son?

**Russell** Not me, Misses.

**Lysette** Shsh, Russ – hear her out.

***Madame Bonneville*** *gestures* ***Russell*** *to move to the foot of the grave.*

**Russell** Me?

**Lysette** Do it, Russ.

*Slowly, uncertainly, **Russell** does as he is asked. He stands at the foot of the grave, his back now to the audience.*

*To heighten the emotion of the moment, music softly and then more assertively accompanies **Madame Bonnneville**'s next words. This is 'The Lark Ascending' by Ralph Vaughan Williams.*

***Madame Bonneville** looks around her at the mourners, then at **Russell**, then into the grave.*

**MME BONNEVILLE** Oh Mr. Paine ... my son stands there as a testament ... to the gratitude of America. *(pause as the music continues)* And I stand here ... for France.

*She has kept a single flower, a rose, till last. She drops it into the grave.*

**LYSETTE** *steps to the very edge of the grave* Tom, this is Lysette, and Russell – and Form 11C. Your friends. *(she looks up towards the audience)* We stand here at long, long last – for Britain.

*Finally, she casts her own flowers into the grave. As one, the mourners turn to the audience, raise their hands in salute. The lights gradually fade as all the characters, except **Lysette** and **Russell**, file off stage.*

*For a few seconds more, Vaughan Williams' lark spirals higher and higher into the sky; then diminishes into silence.*

## Scene 12

*A single spotlight centres on **Lysette** and **Russell** exactly as they were at the beginning of Scene 11, together in a police cell. The cell door opens and the **Jailer** enters. He speaks as a modern policeman.*

**JAILER** All right, you two. Count yourselves damn lucky – you're being released, without charge.

*They get up, suspicious.*

**RUSSELL** No guillotine, then?

**Jailer** Guillotine? What you talking about? You're free.

***Russell** pauses, turns, reaches out as if for Tom Paine's prison door, looks for the number written in chalk. He shakes his head.*

Orders of Inspector Paine.

**Lysette** Inspector *Tom* Paine?

**Jailer** Who cares?

**Russell** We care.

**Jailer** For crying out loud, what does it matter? You're free.

**Lysette** Inspector Tom Paine – oh yes, it matters. It matters a lot.

*They pass the **Jailer**, heading along the front of the stage.*

**Jailer** *calling after them* Friend of your Dad's, is he?

*They pause, half turn towards the **Jailer** and the audience.*

**Lysette** No, Constable. *(she takes **Russell**'s hand. They step to the front of the stage. She addresses the audience and the world)* A friend of the human race!

*For a moment **Lysette** and **Russell** stare out into the audience. Then, together, they smile and bow. It is curtain-call and the rest of the cast enter from stage right and left, clasping hands and bowing to the audience (which hopefully is now applauding).*

*While **Lysette** and **Russell** continue to smile and bow at the front of the stage, the rest of the cast exit into the wings and then return for another curtain-call.*

*They are on the point of leaving the stage for the final time when **Russell** signals for everyone to stop; thus everyone looks confused.*

**Russell** Wait on, you lot! 'Ave y' forgotten item 13 on the agenda? *(he stares at the audience, makes hand gestures to quell the applause)* This audience 'as been kippin' by the looks o'things. *(addresses the audience)* 'Aven't none of you' noticed? – nothin's bin settled.

*Pause, and silence.*

**Lysette** He's right. *(to the cast and to the audience)* We've come all this way, and there's still been no decision – about 'StirCrap', my article, and our website.

**Sonja** Well I've got to get home to take my Gran's tea out the oven. Tuesdays we have chicken kisserole.

**Jackson** *steps forward* Why don't we let the audience decide?

**Lester** Good heavens no – we can't let every Tom, Dick and Deirdre make such an important decision.

***Tony** and **Imran** reach into the wings and bring out two placards. They come forward, holding up the back of the placards to the audience.*

**Lysette** Tom Paine said we should trust the people. *(she signals to **Tony** and **Imran** to display the messages on the placards. Tony's reads BAN & SURVIVE! and **Imran**'s PUBLISH & BE DAMNED! She points to **Tony**'s placard)* That should read BE SERVILE, by the way.

**Julian** *steps forward* It's not that easy. I mean, freedom and responsibility, surely?

**Lester** Very well said, Julian. The damage to the school could be colossal. Colossal!

**Lysette** And what about the damage to us, Headmaster, and to what the school stands for?

**Lester** You'll understand one day. *(he sidles up to **Mrs Draper** who is standing at the front of the stage, by the wings)* Mrs. D? Sound the fire alarm, if you please.

**Mitchell** *stepping into **Mrs. Draper**'s path* Not till we've taken the vote, Mrs. D. That's what we call democracy, isn't it, JackoSir?

**Lester** Mr. Jackson will tell you that democracy does not apply to children. Right, Jesse?

**Jackson** *he shrugs* Well, Headmaster – sometimes I wonder whether it even applies to adults.

**Lester** You would say that!

***Miss Bolton** moves to **Mr Jackson**. She slips her arm through his.*

**Form 11C** *together, as if to confirm and support the evident pairing of their favourite teachers* Aaah!

**Lysette** *to the audience* Okay – point taken. Ladies and gentlemen, if you'll be patient for a moment before rushing off, we'll take that vote. Right, now who's for ? –

*All the lights go out. When they come on again a second later the **Jailer**, now in the guise of the School Caretaker, has come to the front of the stage. He carries a broom in his hand and sweeps towards **Lysette**.*

**Jailer** *to the cast* 'Op off 'ome, you lot. I've a school to get clean for't Inspection. *(to the audience)* And you, y'can do yer discussin' an' yer votin' outside. Stir yer stumps. Otherwise it's… *(he makes the sign of a throat being cut. He chuckles, points upwards – and we hear once again the swish and fall of the guillotine)* Get me meanin'?

*Now all the cast reassemble in a line. They smile and begin to clap the audience; hopefully, before departing, the audience will applaud the cast.*

# *Staging the play*

This is what the author James Watson says about the staging of the play:

"In this play, time and location are flexible – past and present, here and elsewhere, merging into one another with a view to the drama happening in the head rather than on the hard surfaces of a stage. Essentially this is a journey of the imagination, for the actors and for the audience.

Chiefly, if the play is to be produced as well as read in class, the effects will be created by lighting. The stage should really be as empty of scenery and props as possible. Imagination is the stage, it needs only modest prompting.

Even so, some props will be essential. I would suggest easily moveable boxes which can be swiftly shifted into different positions, and a couple of large step-ladders. These will serve as an arch, rising out of an old ruin, located in the grounds of William Pitt School, and as steps to the guillotine in later scenes of the play.

## ACTING STYLE

The play's language demands a pacey, upfront delivery of lines. A lot of the comedy is in both the language and in the comic contrast of the figures of authority and their levels of incompetence. The acting should become quite heightened at times, even cartoon-like. Look at scene 6 33
set in the TV studio: what should the actor playing Jethro Jackson do to help him 'become' the TV show host? Should he have an American accent?

Exaggerating some of the lines and the action for comic effect can help highlight some of the really funny moments in the play. For example, in Scene 1 p17, this piece of dialogue can be made very 17
melodramatic and over the top with the actors freezing in postures of terror and alarm after each line. In small groups, try this out and then share your work with the rest of the group.

## THE STAGE

Though the play could be performed in a classroom, given that most of the play is set in a present day school, it would be better to have access to a large hall or drama studio. The set is quite carefully specified by the author. He suggests a very simple, stripped down set that is not making any attempt to be realistic, so a ruined archway can be represented by a couple of stepladders joined by a plank; seats in a TV studio or chairs in a classroom can be represented by, as the author says, 'a couple of sturdy boxes a metre or so square, half a metre deep.'

The type of staging used will also affect the pace and the look and feel of the production. For example, a proscenium arch staging would help the director create strong pictures with the large cast. Different levels can be used to help sightlines and audibility. But if the play was staged in the round, with the audience on three or four sides, scenes can begin as cast members walk though the audience to the central playing area. The advantage of this staging is that the audience can feel much more part of the action: for example, when the TV scene takes place, the cast audience could sit in amongst the real audience. The tempo of the play would be faster as the scenes flow into each other, but careful consideration would have to be given to how well the players can be seen and heard and to giving equal weighting to each section of the audience.

If you opt for a more traditional staging, with the audience 'out front', you can create a raised dais at the rear of the acting area which will help not just with sightlines but also with creating different effects. When Lysette and Julian express their conflicting opinions in Scene 10, they could stand on the dais so it becomes almost like a political debate, with 11C and the teachers and Lady Testard heckling and counter-arguing from the floor. However you decide to stage *Banned! Tom Paine, This Was Your Life*, bear in mind that the set and props need to be very flexible and in keeping with the style of the play.

## LIGHTING

Lighting can be effective in delineating the acting space and signalling a change in mood or pace within the play. In most scenes the lights are very naturalistic, but in those where Thomas Paine appears he could have his own pale blue spotlight to create an ethereal, other worldly effect. In Scene 6, set in the TV studio, the lights should dim and a spotlight be used to pick out the guests on the show. Gobos – shapes cut out of metal – can be placed in front of lights to create the effect of shadows. Rather than wheeling on a piece of scenery to depict the prison scenes, a gobo could cast 'prison bar' shadows across the playing area.

## MUSIC & SOUND EFFECTS

Music is also very useful in order to create mood or anticipate the arrival of a key character. Try to think of ways of making music that don't depend on using recorded music. Incidental sounds can be made by the actors themselves, e.g. whistling wind in Scene 5 when Thomas Paine appears, and shouts and cries 'outside' the cell in Scene 7. Go through the play carefully to check where and when the author specifies particular music. The one point at which recorded music can be used to cover up the activity surrounding the re-setting of boxes, TV cameras etc. is between Scenes 5 and 6 when some big band style, rather cheesy TV theme tune could be played, helping to set the scene.

A very specific sound effect that is used is that of the swish and fall of a guillotine. You may have to use a sound effects record for this.

## COSTUMES

Obviously most of the cast wears school uniform throughout. The characters from Thomas Paine's time should wear period costume if at all possible. If parts are doubled up, then using a shawl for Mme Bonneville or a leather jerkin for the jailer may be all you need for a quick turnaround between scenes.

# *Work on and around the script*

## THE CHARACTERS

All the characters in this play are very well-defined, both by what the author tells us about them in the cast list as well as by what they say. If you are all the same age, you need to cast the older characters carefully so that the audience can believe that they really are adults. This is especially true of those playing adults with quite a lot of authority, even if they are also figures of fun such as Hector Lester, the Headmaster, and Lady Testard. The humour will come from the contrast between the recognition of their authority and the silliness of what they say and do.

Characters can be developed by making notes about such things as how they sound and move, who they feel most comfortable with, what they like and dislike. As an example, this has been done below for the character of Jethro Jackson. The author's notes are followed by further ideas suggested by a reading of the play:

**Jethro Jackson** History master, probationary teacher; popular with his students; form master for 11C.

| Name | History | Likes | Dislikes | Distinctive Features |
|---|---|---|---|---|
| Jethro Jackson | Second generation child of parents who came to the UK from the Caribbean. Won scholarship to Oxford where he studied for a PhD. | History and particularly admires men and women of principle who have stood up for their beliefs, 11C (sometimes!) and Miss Bolton. | Some aspects of the school system. Having fun made of him by his class. | A patience and willingness to listen to his pupils. Serious demeanour. Good posture. Clear and well-spoken voice, almost sounds 'posh'. |
| | | | | |

The author has made notes on each of the parts that have lines; here are the full descriptions of Hector Lester, Lysette and Miss Bolton:

**Hector Lester** Headmaster, William Pitt School. A mixture of the authoritarian and the stressed humanitarian. Genuinely terrified of the imminent inspection of the school and mortified by the comments in the article written by LYSETTE. He is so overworked and up-tight that he fails to remember the correct names of his staff; is peremptory yet has the minor saving grace of being able to remember better days when teaching and learning were no longer the mechanised, league-table-driven exercise they seem to have become.

**Lysette** Central character of the play, Lysette is editor of the controversial Form 11C section of the school magazine and author of the article that has caused such a rumpus in the school, 'Pitt School is Pants!'

She is a deeply sceptical person but also passionate about a number of concerns. She is inflamed at the prospect of her work being censored. She lives on a short fuse. But for discovering an interest in writing she would have been a school dropout. Having realised that interest – and talent – she shows the commitment of a revolutionary; in doing so, she inspires RUSSELL.

**Lorna Bolton** English teacher. Young, new to the job; her ideals concerning education and the treatment of her pupils always seem to run counter to the expectations of those in authority. She remembers her own school experience and in her own teaching tries to turn that experience around – being more friendly and supportive to those in her charge. At the same time she admires rebels rather than being one herself.

## Character Profiles

**In pairs**

*Select one of the above three characters and provide a fuller description of them in a table, using the notes on Jethro Jackson as a model. Draw both on your reading of the play and your imagination to make up the missing detail.*

cont...

**On your own**

H Select one other character from the play; this should be the one you are playing if you are performing the script. Repeat the same note-taking exercise to deepen your understanding.

Share your notes with the rest of the class. Can anything be added?

## Drama

Sometimes improvising scenes that are similar to the ones included in the play can clarify a character's motivation. The confrontations between Julian and Lysette may become stronger and clearer if the performers use their own words and arguments.

**A.** *Organisation:* Work with a partner. One of you is Lysette and the other is Julian.

*Situation:* Lysette and Julian meet privately to discuss her article.

*Opening line:* **JULIAN:** Look Lysette, I think you've written a really interesting piece but if you insist on publishing it, we, not the school, will suffer.

**B.** *Organisation:* Work in pairs.

*Situation:* Looking into the future, Lysette has become an activist on behalf of the rights of young people. She is being interviewed by a radio station.

*Opening line:* **INTERVIEWER:** Welcome Lysette. We all know about your work over the past few years. I believe you are now an advisor to the government and there is talk of you standing for Parliament. Can you tell the listeners what first got you interested in human and civil rights?

Other useful exercises for building backgrounds to the characters can be created by improvising scenes that are not included in the play.

**C.** *Organisation:* Work in a group of three or four. One of you is Jackson and the others are more experienced members of the school staff.

*Situation:* His colleagues give Jackson advice about how to handle the different personalities in his classroom.

Opening line: TEACHER: You have to be firm with them – don't let them get the upper hand.

**D.** *Organisation:* Work in pairs

*Situation:* Before meeting the Headmaster, Jackson and Miss Bolton are discussing Lysette's article.

*Opening lines:* **MISS BOLTON:** You have to back me up. I've rewritten the article and I think she has the right to have it published.

**JACKSON:** I agree, Lorna. But you've been writing 11C's coursework too. You have to let them – and Lysette – stand on their own two feet.

## Hot Seating

*Situation:* Take each of the cast who is playing a member of form 11C and 'hot seat' them. They are interviewed in turn about their response to the events in the play, their background, their solution to the 'publish and be damned' issue and their feelings about the other characters such as Thomas Paine, Miss Bolton and Lady Testard. At the end of each questioning session, ask them to summarise their own personal journey from the start to the finish of the play.

## Writing



**A.** Imagine that you are Mr. Jackson. You are writing a letter to a friend about your new job. How will you describe the different personalities in your class? Will you reveal your real feelings about each of them? Alternatively, you might choose to write a diary extract, describing the events in the first scene of the play.

**B.** Imagine that you are another teacher in the school. Decide what subject you teach. Write an end of term report for three of the members of 11C. How does each one behave in your lessons? What is your relationship like with each of them? Do they achieve anything in your lessons?

**C.** Choose one of the members of 11C, other than Lysette. Think about what they might become when they leave school. Write a brief biography for them, outlining their future career.

## AUTHORITY AND STATUS

Several moments in the play are about challenging authority, from a minor way in petty classroom interruptions that occur at the start of the play, right through to the final scenes when the pupils have imprisoned the Headmaster, the school governor and the teachers. The main theme of the play is the importance of challenging accepted ideas or ways of seeing or doing things. This is seen both in Lysette's struggle to get her article published, and in the inspirational figure of Thomas Paine who was instrumental in the ideas that challenged the authorities of his day.

### Research

Authority figures usually have what is known as 'high' status, but in the play this can change as it progresses. Lysette stays pretty much the same; her confidence is always high, she is a natural leader. Hector Lester, on the other hand, changes quite a bit and he always seems to find it a struggle to maintain his status.

*On your own*

H Select one of the following characters: Jethro Jackson, Lady Testard, Hector Lester, Julian Hicks, Lysette. Chart the way the character's status alters over the course of the drama by picking out the key incidents that show the character's level of authority and status. When you have collected about 7 such incidents, plot them on a line graph using the vertical axis to show increasing level of status, and the horizontal axis to show the play's movement in time.

How authoritative is your character? How do you account for the constant or changing level of authority they have?

## WILLIAM PITT SCHOOL

The play highlights a host of problems that confront the school just prior to its inspection. It is on account of these that the Headmaster reacts with such comic horror when he believes an inspector has arrived in disguise.

## Discussion and Writing

**In pairs**

Make a list of all the problems that the school has.

Now imagine that you were in charge of the school. Which problems are most serious? How would you deal with each problem?

**On your own**

The following writing tasks require you to think carefully about the style appropriate for each activity. Remember that the style of your writing is determined by the purpose and intended reader of the piece.

**A.** As head of William Pitt School, design and write an advertisement for the local paper. Its purpose is to attract parents to sending their children to the school.

**B.** Imagine that you are the parent of a year 11 student. You have heard things about the school that have worried you in the light of your child's forthcoming examinations. Write a letter to the Headmaster in which you raise your concerns about the running of the school.

**C.** Imagine the school was inspected. What problems would be spotted? Write the report on the school. This should include a brief summary of the main weaknesses (and any strengths) and then a list of the main problems. Beside each problem write the action which the school needs to take to remedy it. The document will be for the teachers and governors.

# *Themes in and around the play*

## THOMAS PAINE

Before looking at the play's main themes, it might be asked why a red-nosed, hard-drinking man, born as long ago as 1737, should win such a central part in a 21st century play. Hopefully the play itself begins to answer this question by showing how the ideas and the visions of men and women in our past can powerfully influence the present, though at first we may not suspect this.

Jethro Jackson calls Paine the 'father of human rights' and the 'greatest Englishman'. He published many political pamphlets in which he argued for democratically elected governments to replace the rule of monarchies. His views were very popular with the people and unpopular with the rich and powerful.

As the play makes clear, Paine influenced the American War of Independence and the subsequent establishment of the world's first great democracy. His influence upon the French Revolution was equally profound. When he returned to England from America in 1787, he published *The Rights of Man*, a spirited response to Edmund Burke's critical *Reflections on the Revolution in France* ( which is why the vindictive Mrs Burke appears in the play).

*The Rights of Man* sold an estimated 100,000–200,000 copies in the first three years of publication and ranks among the finest works on politics, liberty, equality and justice that have ever been published. Paine's influence was so great, that a new national anthem was written in praise of him.

It might seem strange, then, that Tom Paine is so little known either in Britain or, indeed, in the United States. The play suggests why this might be so; it also argues that it is high time the great man got his due.

The section that follows will help you to explore Paine's influence on human rights and democracy, both in this country and abroad.

## HUMAN RIGHTS AND DEMOCRACY

As we have seen, Paine had a great influence on the establishment of democracies in both America and France.

The series of dates below show some of the main turning points in the development of human rights, beginning with the publication of Paine's *Rights of Man*. The work that follows, and the resources listed at the back of the book, will help you to find out more about each event and understand the influence of a man like Tom Paine.

### Human Rights and Democracy Timeline – from Thomas Paine to the present day

1791
Thomas Paine publishes *Rights of Man*

1792
Mary Wollstonecraft publishes *A Vindication of the Rights of Women*, widely considered the first feminst tract

1833
Slavery is abolished in British empire

1865
Slavery abolished in US

1920
Extension of female vote in UK

1948
The United Nations approves the Universal Declaration of Human Rights, guaranteeing all people in all countries their basic rights

1975
UK passes Sex Discrimination Act

1989
Fall of the Berlin Wall

Popular student-led, pro-democracy protests take place in Beijing's Tiananmen Square, sparking Chinese government crackdown

1991
The Soviet Union disintegrates as the Communist Party loses power; democratic elections are held in Russia and throughout Eastern Europe

## Research and Drama

In small groups, research one of the key events using the resources at the back of the book and your school library. You should aim to be able to answer the questions below:

H

- What happened?
- What changes did it bring for people and why was it so important?
- Why did it happen when it did?

Illustrate your key event so the rest of your class can understand its importance. You can use a variety of methods: either create a series of tableaux that illustrate the progress of a particular development in the growth of democracy, or present your chosen date/incident by interviewing witnesses at the scene in the manner of a TV reporter.

**Example – Civil Rights**

*Tableau I* – Rosa Parks refuse to give up her seat and sit in the 'black' section of the bus

*Tableau II* – Marches and protests

*Tableau III* – Martin Luther King speaking to audience

*Tableau IV* – Martin Luther King's assassination

*Between 1789 and 1795 the French Revolution transformed France. Feudalism and the monarchy were abolished in the creation of a republic. In 1793 King Louis XVI of France was executed by guillotine. Many thousands of people suffered the same fate in the ensuing months.*

In 1948 the United Nations drew up the *Universal Declaration of Human Rights*. The document contains 30 articles designed to promote and defend the rights and freedoms of all peoples in all nations. Article 19 is the right which the play is most concerned with:

> 'Everyone has the right to freedom of opinion and expression; this right includes freedom to hold opinions without interference and to seek, receive and impart information and ideas through any media and regardless of frontiers'.

The play explores the conflict which arises when one group of people have their views suppressed.

### Discussion

Schools are run by teachers, who in turn are responsible to both the board of governors and to parents. Where do you, the pupil, fit in to the school system?

**In groups**

- How much of a democracy do you think school is? Is it simply a case of the minority (teachers) making all the decisions? Are there forums for your views to be expressed, such as a school council, year representatives, or a school magazine? Do you have any say in the rules or the code of conduct?
- Do rules run counter to democracy and freedom?
- According to the events of the play and your own experience, what problems arise when rules are abandoned?

## IDEALS AND COMPROMISE

In the play Jethro Jackson is faced with the dilemma of standing up for his beliefs in freedom of speech or bowing to the pressures from the Headmaster.

As an ardent fan of Tom Paine, he declares to Lysette and 11C that he believes in freedom of speech (see p15) and promises to try to help them in their fight to have Lysette's article published. Yet as a new teacher he is called upon by the Headmaster to convince the class that the article should at least be postponed until after the inspection. Has he weakly sacrificed his ideals, or is he right to act as he does?

This question is explored further later in the play when Lorna Bolton speaks of the struggle to stand up for one's beliefs:

---

> Poor Tom, the world has never forgiven you. I'm beginning to know how you must have felt. You can speak the truth too much for your own good.

---

## Research and Discussion

**In groups of 4 or 6**

**A.** Divide up the following sections of the script within your group, with a pair of you working on two or three of the sections. In all of these we learn something new about Jackson's beliefs and ideals and how they fare under pressure.

1 pp14–17
2 pp19–22
3 pp35, 37–39
4 pp48–52
5 pp57–58
6 72–75, 77–78

Each pair should read through their sections and discuss and make notes on Jackson. What do we learn about his beliefs? Why does he admire Tom Paine? Does he support and stand up for 11C? Does he say what he believes or do you think he is forced to compromise?

**B.** When each pair has finished their research, share your findings with the rest of your group. How and why does Jackson change?

**As a class**

**C.** Do you think the author encourages us to sympathise with Jackson or not? What is your response to him? Do you think he has acted responsibly, or has he failed to live up to his beliefs?

### Writing

Imagine that certain characters kept a diary of the events that took place during Lady Testard's meeting at the school (scene 10).

Take the character of Hector Lester, Jethro Jackson or Lady Testard and write their account of the events. Consider whether on reflection they regret any of their actions or decisions. Do they believe they did the right thing?

60

H

### Writing

**On your own**

Can you think of examples from your own experience when you have been under pressure to act in a way that went against your beliefs of what is right and wrong?

Write about these occasions, trying to explain clearly how you felt and why you acted the way you did. What were the outcomes of your actions? Do you think you would act in the same way again?

H

## CENSORSHIP

One of the main themes in the play is the issue of censorship. Lysette and her classmates feel that by others altering her article and then refusing to publish it, they are the victims of censorship.

### Discussion

**A.** In small groups, try and come up with a sentence or short paragraph that defines 'censorship'. Does it apply only to things that are published or is behaviour subject to censorship? Check your answers against the dictionary definition.

**B.** What examples of censorship can you find around you in daily life? Is not being allowed to see an 18 film when you are only 15 censorship? Make a list of as many examples as you can think of.

How far do you agree that censorship exists to protect you from harm, or is it about people in authority, such as the police or politicians, trying to control ideas and behaviour?

## Research

23

If you have access to the internet you can look at the two versions of Lysette's article for *Forward*, her school magazine. Her article entitled *Pitt School is Pants!*, and Miss Bolton's version, entitled *Is School as Good as the Press Claim?*, can both be found by following the link at www.collinseducation.com/Banned

**A.** Besides differences in spelling and punctuation, what other differences are there between the two versions? Consider the content, the style and the tone of each.

**B.** Select four examples from the two articles of where the same point has been expressed in two very different ways. How is the language different in each version? Has the rewording of Lysette's resulted in a different implication or suggestion being conveyed?

## CIVIL RIGHTS

Here is an article about the possible infringement of civil rights that comes about through extensive use of technology:

---

"How would you feel if your children's fingerprints were being taken at school, without your knowledge or consent, and stored on computer?...

Privacy International, an admirable human rights organisation, recently received a complaint from the mother of an 11-year-old child attending a London primary school.

She had discovered that all the pupils had been electronically finger-printed for a new library management system. The school had not asked the parents for their consent, nor were the children given an explanation of their legal rights.

PI investigated the complaint and discovered that the fingerprinting system has been sold to a thousand British schools, resulting in the fingerprinting of as many as 200,000 children.

According to PI, the technology is similar to the identification systems used in US prisons and by the German military. It is being employed in our schools – sometimes in conjunction with digitised photographs – to replace library cards and to increase the efficiency of library management. Each child is required to place a thumb onto an electronic scanner, and the identity of the print is then stored in a computer.

It would be tempting to interpret this latest triumph of information technology as part of a sinister plot to soften up British youngsters for ID cards and electronic tagging. Tempting, but wrong. In fact, the fingerprinting system provides a graphic illustration of how institutions and companies attempting to solve a practical problem – the infuriating tendency of school kids to lose or mutilate their library cards – can opt for a technological solution which thoughtlessly erodes privacy and infringes civil rights".

John Naughton, *The Observer*, 28th July, 2002

Read the following article:

## NURSERIES FIT ELECTRONIC TAGS TO CHILDREN

Thousands of schoolchildren as young as three are being fitted with electronic security tags used to monitor psychiatric patients as fears over child abductions and safety increase.

As many as 100 schools have now provided children with these new devices. They have been adapted from tags used on clothes to prevent high street theft.

Childcare groups and charities have accused security companies of trying to cash in on schools' fears over pupil safety. "More and more high-tech security options are coming into the nursery market. This is led by security companies seeing a marketing opportunity rather than demand from the sector," said Rosemary Murphy, chief executive of the National Day Nurseries Association. "Nursery managers should think carefully about their nursery's needs before they commit to expensive investment."

Electronic tags are already used to monitor mental patients in hospitals and offenders on probation.

In schools, children are told to carry them in their pockets or play overalls. The device emits a high-pitched bleep when the child passes electronic receiver posts at school exit gates. The system costs between £2,000 and £3,000 and a disposable tag costs between £2 and forty pence'.

Sophie Goodchild and Claire Newbon, *The Independent*, 26 May 2002

## Drama

**In pairs**

*Situation:* In pairs, A & B. A is the parent or carer and B a young person of 14. Scientists have invented an implant that is inserted under the skin and is invisible.

*Opening lines:* **A**: Oh good. I'm glad I've bumped into you. We decided, in conjunction with the school and with the police, that it would be best if you and your friends had an electronic implant. That way, we'll know exactly where you are and we won't be worried about you.

**B**: But I don't want to have one. It's my body. Besides, it won't stop me being kidnapped will it?

Continue the exercise with A arguing for B to have the implant. Then do the same exercise again, but swap roles and this time make Child B younger. Do the arguments change because the child is younger?

## Drama and Writing

**As a class**

*Situation:* Half of the group to take roles such as police inspectors, teachers, parents, social workers, prison officers; the others to be young people of various ages and backgrounds who will be interviewed in front of the panel.

Those playing grown ups are a panel of experts. Each child is assessed for their suitability and willingness to have an electronic implant. There are only enough implants for half the children to have one.

The experts should think about what they would need to know for the purposes of assessment. Would a social worker be able to identify a particularly 'at risk' child? Would the policeman or woman see these implants as a version of the electronic tagging used on young offenders and be keen for potential troublemakers to have the implants?

*Opening lines:* **SPOKESPERSON**: I know some of you are here because you want the electronic implant so that you will feel safer, and therefore freer, when you are out playing. And some of you resent the implication that you cannot look after yourselves, or spot potential danger. Well there are only enough of these expensive implants for half of you. That means we have to assess each case and consult with each other before making a decision.

**Extension**

**A.** The experts should collaborate on writing a half page report on each child who comes before them. This will mean taking notes during the assessment.

**B.** Imagine you have had the implant: write a week long diary describing how it does – or doesn't – change you life.

H

# *Research resources and further reading*

**Web Resources:**

Thomas Paine:
http://www.bbc.co.uk/history/society_culture/protest_reform/paine_01.shtml

Mary Wollstonecraft:
http://www.bbc.co.uk/history/society_culture/protest_reform/wollstonecraft_01.shtml

Definitions of government:
http://news.bbc.co.uk/cbbcnews/hi/find_out/guides/world/united_nations/types_of_government/newsid_2151000/2151570.stm

Civil Rights:
http://www.civilrights.org/

Human Rights Watch: www.hrw.org

The site for Liberty, a group that defends human rights and civil liberties in the UK: http://www.liberty-human-rights.org.uk/

Privacy International – a human rights group formed in 1990 as a watchdog on surveillance by governments and corporations: http://www.privacyinternational.org/

An organization that campaigns against the perceived erosion of democracy: http://www.charter88.org.uk/

Campaign for Racial Equality:
http://www.cre.gov.uk/

**Further reading:**

*Antigone* by Aeschylus

*The Ubu Plays* by Alfred Jarry

*A Tale of Two Cities* by Charles Dickens

# Activities Mapping

English Framework Objectives (Year 7/8/9)

| Page Number | Learning Objectives (Year 7/8/9) | | | |
|---|---|---|---|---|
| | Word (W) & Sentence (S) Level | Text Level | | Speaking & Listening |
| | | Reading | Writing | |
| 93 | | **(7)** 1, 2, 8 | | |
| 94 | | **(7)** 1, 2, 8 | | |
| 94/5 | | | | **(7)** 15, 16, 17, 18<br>**(8)** 14, 15, 16 |
| 95 | **(7)** S12, S13, S15, S17<br>**(8)** W12 | **(7)** 1, 2, 8 | **(7)** 9, 10, 14 | **(7)** 7 |
| 96 | | **(7)** 1, 2, 8<br>**(8)** 3 | **(7)** 2 | |
| 97 | **(7)** S13, S14, S15, S17<br>**(8)** W12; S9<br>**(9)** S3 | **(7)** 1, 2, 8 | **(7)** 2, 12, 16<br>**(8)** 2, 10, 13, 14<br>**(9)** 13 | |
| 100 | | **(7)** 1, 2, 4, 5<br>**(8)** 2 | | **(7)** 16<br>**(8)** 15 |
| 101 | | | | **(7)** 11, 12, 14<br>**(8)** 10, 11, 12 |
| 102 | | **(7)** 1, 2, 4, 6, 8, 9, 16<br>**(8)** 7 | | |

# ACTIVITIES MAPPING – *continued*

| Page Number | Learning Objectives (Year 7/8/9) | | | |
|---|---|---|---|---|
| | Word (W) & Sentence (S) Level | Text Level | | Speaking & Listening |
| | | Reading | Writing | |
| 102/3 | **(7)** W12, W15; S13, S15<br>**(8)** S12 | **(7)** 1, 2, 8 | **(7)** 6, 9, 11<br>**(8)** 7 | **(7)** 1, 5, 7, 11, 13<br>**(8)** 5, 10, 11, 12<br>**(9)** 5, 9 |
| 104 | **(8)** W8, W11, W12, W13; S2, S12<br>**(9)** W6, W7, W8 | **7)** 7, 8, 12, 14<br>**(8)** 3, 6, 7, 8,<br>**(9)** 7, 12 | | |
| 106/7 | **(7)** S13, S15, S17<br>**(8)** W12; S9 | | **(7)** 2, 6, 10, 14 | **(7)** 15, 16, 17, 18<br>**(8)** 14, 15, 16 |

Collins Plays Plus

Other titles in the **Collins** Plays Plus series that you might enjoy:

## *The Tulip Touch*

ANNE FINE

A stunning adaptation by the author of the best-selling novel featuring the story of a disturbed teenager.
*Themes:* Juvenile crime; growing up and friendship
*Cast:* 22 characters (plus extras)

ISBN 0 00 713086 4

## *The Book of the Banshee*

ANNE FINE

Adapted by Anne Fine from her popular novel, this is the story of teenage rebellion and its effects on a family.
*Themes:* Gender roles; family; growing up; pacifism and rebellion
*Cast:* 6 characters

ISBN 0 00 330310 1

## *Flour Babies*

ANNE FINE

The amusing and moving adaptation of the novel exploring one boy's attempt to come to terms with his absent father through a school project on parenting.
*Themes:* Parenting; family
*Cast:* 19 characters

ISBN 0 00 330312 8

## *The Granny Project*

ANNE FINE

When Ivan finds himself responsible for looking after his grandmother single-handedly he finds he has more than he had bargained for. The play is a humorous take on family roles and sensitively explores the issue of ageism.
*Themes:* Ageism; family roles; parenting
*Cast:* 7 characters

ISBN 0 00 330234 2

## *The Birds Keep on Singing*

STEPHEN COCKETT

The story of three evacuees billeted with two sisters during World War II. As the adults struggle to cope, the children come to a truce of their own.
*Themes:* War; relationships
*Cast:* 11 characters

ISBN 0 00 330315 2

## *Dear Nobody*

BERLIE DOHERTY

Adapted from the award-winning book, this play examines how two teenagers cope with an unplanned pregnancy.
*Themes:* Teenage pregnancy; relationships; growing up
*Cast:* 16 characters

ISBN 0 00 320004 3

## *Black Harvest*

NIGEL GRAY

A tense and gripping drama set on the rugged west coast of Ireland. A fun family holiday goes horribly wrong when the horrors of the Irish potato famine return to haunt them.
*Themes*: Famine
*Cast*: 10 characters

ISBN 0 00 330233 4